Encounters with the World's Religions

Encounters with the
World's Religions

The Numinous on Highway 395

BRAD KARELIUS

WIPF & STOCK · Eugene, Oregon

ENCOUNTERS WITH THE WORLD'S RELIGIONS
The Numinous on Highway 395

Wipf & Stock
An Imprint of Wipf and Stock Publishers
199 W. 8th Ave., Suite 3
Eugene, OR 97401

www.wipfandstock.com

ISBN 13: 978-1-4982-0002-8

Manufactured in the U.S.A.   05/12/2015

*This book is written in thanksgiving for
the students in my classes on world religion
at Saddleback College, Mission Viejo, California, 1973–2013*

To the desert go prophets and hermits; through deserts go pilgrims and exiles. Here the leaders of the great religions have sought the therapeutic and spiritual values of retreat, not to escape, but to find reality.

—Paul Shephard, *Man in the Landscape: A Historic View of the Aesthetics of Nature*

Contents

Acknowledgments

THANK YOU TO THOSE who read the manuscript and offered important criticism and ideas: Dr. Walter Brueggemann of Columbia Theological Seminary; Dr. Jack Miles of the University of California at Irvine; Father James Martin, SJ; Dr. Francis X. Clooney, SJ, of the Harvard Center for the Study of World Religions; Dr. Denise Carmody of Santa Clara University; Sr. Eileen McNerney of the Sisters of St. Joseph of Orange; Dr. Lawrence Budner, MD; Chris Langley of the Lone Pine Film History Museum; and Brenda Lacey of Lacey Ranch, Independence, California.

I am grateful for my spiritual director, Fr. Gordon Moreland, SJ, of the House of Prayer in the Roman Catholic Diocese of Orange, California. His prayerful encouragement has guided me through many interior deserts over the past twenty years.

Thank you to Jon Klusmire and Roberta Harlan of the Eastern California Museum, Independence, California, for help with the historical photographs in this book. Sincere appreciation to David Thunder Eagle, Interim Tribal Administrator for the Bishop Paiute Tribe, and to Ms. Mary Wuester, Chairperson of the Lone Pine Paiute Tribe, for reviewing the manuscript of this book.

Thank you to my philosophy students at Saddleback Community College, Mission Viejo, California, for what you have shared with me in your spiritual journeys. I am grateful for my Dean, Dr. Kevin O'Connor, and for my Department Chair, Dr. Basil Smith, for the privilege of being a teacher on the subject of the world's religions. I am grateful for my mentor and teacher, Huston Smith of the University of California at Berkeley.

Finally, thank you to Denis Clarke and Source Books. Denis is the copy editor of this book and lovingly polished the rough work. Over the years, we have shared a ministry with the poor and homeless in Santa Ana and I am blessed to have had his participation in this project.

ACKNOWLEDGMENTS

~ * ~

Every effort has been made to trace the holders of copyrighted material used in this book. The author is grateful for permission to quote from the following:

The Gift: Poems by the Great Sufi Master, translated by Daniel Ladinsky. Copyright © 1999 Daniel Ladinsky. Used by permission.

Special appreciation goes to Zane Grey, Inc. for permission to quote from *Desert Gold*, by Zane Grey, copyright © 1913.

Thank you to Chris Langley for permission to quote him from personal conversation and from his article "Living in the Land of 20 Mile Shadows," in *Territorial Review Monthly*, November 2008.

Thank you to the Eastern California Museum of the County of Inyo, California , for permission to reproduce photos from their extensive file of historic photographs.

Thank you to Lawrence Budner, MD, for his explanation of constructing the False Self in chapter 9.

"Religious Practice: Rite, Myth, and Meditation," part 1, "Hindu Perspectives," by Heinrich von Stietencron. In *Christianity and the World Religions*, by Hans Küng et al. Copyright © 1986 Doubleday and Company, Inc. Used by permission of Orbis Books.

At Home in the Cosmos, by David Toolan, SJ, copyright © 2001. Used by permission of Orbis Books.

Several articles by Father Ron Rolheiser, OMI, from his personal blog, at http://ronrolheiser.com. Used by permission.

"Ah, Not to Be Cut Off," by Rainer Maria Rilke, translation by Stephen Mitchell. In *Ahead of All Parting: The Selected Poetry and Prose of Rainer Maria Rilke*, translated and edited by Stephen Mitchell. Translation copyright © 1995 Stephen Mitchell. Used by permission of Modern Library, an imprint of Random House, a division of Random House, LLC. All rights reserved. Any third party use of this material outside of this publication is prohibited. Interested parties must apply directly to Random House LLC for permission.

Brief quotations from pp. 61, 65 (stand alone) and p. 190 (epigraph) of *The Wisdom of the Wilderness: Experiencing the Healing Power of Nature*, by Gerald G. May, copyright ©2006. Used by permission of Harper Collins Publishers.

Chapters 3, 8, and 25 from *Tao Te Ching*, by Lao Tzu, translated by Stephen Mitchell. Translation copyright ©1988 Stephen Mitchell. Used by permission of Harper Collins Publishers.

Prelude

Foundational Experiences in the Desert

I will draw you out to the desert and I will speak to your heart.
—HOSEA 2:14

SUMMER MOONLIGHT FILTERS THROUGH the bedroom window, illuminating the face of our sleeping son, Erik. His face glows in radiant peace: a child's face on the body of a twenty-nine-year-old man.

Twenty-five years ago encephalitis ravaged Erik's body with relentless fever. In and out of coma at Massachusetts General Hospital, Erik survived. Scars cored deep into his brain, leaving him prone to constant seizures. He has suffered immense pain and distress, but still he lives, and for the moment he sleeps in peace.

As I lie on my bed next to his, I contemplate the events of the day. From waking, through all the encounters with people, the stream of thoughts flows through my mind. I lift my heart to God in thanksgiving for small graces and I ask pardon for insensitivities or harm done, known and unknown.

My thoughts shift to the California desert. I am driving north on Highway 395, past the intersection with Highway 58 at Kramer Junction. Dawn breaks with crimson clouds blanketing purple mountains and a golden sheen covers the sagebrush. I stop my car and walk east into the desert, a hundred yards or so beyond the sounds of the highway. Facing east in this land without fences, I can see at least fifty miles into a sagebrush ocean. Something stirs my heart in this place. I have encountered the Presence again. Like a bed sheet hung on a clothesline, my soul opens up as the wind of the Spirit flows through me. I lift my arms in praise for this new day. I sense I am surrounded by love and peace and joy and hope.

It is certainly a religious feeling, but not a feeling you could ascribe to a particular religion. The Christian ecumenist James Nash describes it well:

> The so-called desert is any place of solitude, simplicity and emptiness—a barren wasteland, figuratively—to which one withdraws for undistracted communication with God. One closes one's eyes and blocks out the other senses in order to experience the Spirit with utmost clarity. The process is seemingly transcendental rather than sacramental.[1]

This is one of my foundational encounters with God in the desert. It comes back to me frequently in these moments of contemplation before I sleep. It is something that happened in the past, but it lives in my soul, and remembering brings me back to this present moment, this present breath, this communion with the Holy. Hope, love, joy, and peace fill this bedroom, shining with summer moonlight and the beautiful image of Erik sleeping in peace.

1. Nash, *Loving Nature*, 159.

1

Roadside Shrines, Remember Me

We say that the hour of death is uncertain, but when we say this we think of that hour as situated in an obscure and distant future. It does not occur to us that I can have any connection with the day already begun or that death could arrive this same afternoon, this afternoon which is so certain and which has every hour filled in advance.

—MARCEL PROUST[1]

All human experience is narrative in the way we imaginatively reconstruct it . . . and every encounter of the sacred is rooted in a place, a socio-spatial context that is rich in myth and symbol.

—BELDEN LANE[2]

A LADYBUG DRINKS FROM a water droplet on a ripe zucchini in my vegetable plot. I gently lift the garden helpmate onto another plant as I harvest the squash for dinner. Fog moves in from the ocean, flowing over the hills near our home in Laguna Niguel, California. It is an October afternoon, autumn light glows orange and yellow. They say Southern California has no seasons, but it feels as though the transition toward autumn is happening now. There is a distinct smell in the air and softer light in the sunset. Darkness comes more quickly.

1. Proust, *Guermantes Way*, 312.
2. Lane, "Galesville and Sinai."

The sudden sound of a horrific crash and splintering glass thunders a few blocks way. Another accident on busy Crown Valley Parkway, where teen drivers race recklessly. Silence, then the sound of fire trucks and ambulances. Three hours later, my wife, Janice, returns from her work as nurse practitioner in the emergency room at Mission Hospital in Laguna Beach. She confirms that an accident has claimed the life of another young driver. He was probably driving too fast and hit a tree.

I forgot about this until two days later. Driving down the hill towards the intersection with Crown Valley, a surrealistic scene across the street caught my attention. I waited at the signal and could take in more detail. At least fifty high-schoolers were gathered in a tight cluster, shocked faces, crying. Two girls knelt beside a large votive candle burning on the sidewalk. This is where the young man died. Here are his friends.

In the *Los Angeles Times* a story appeared about the driver, a senior at Serra Catholic High School in San Juan Capistrano. There was a brief description about the probable cause, with most of the narrative a collage of remembrances from his classmates.

Many people have died on Crown Valley Parkway and, typically, flowers mark the spot for a few days, to be soon removed by the CalTrans Authority. But this vigil lasted for weeks. Every night, as I waited at the signal to turn homeward, I could see a new demonstration of tender love and friendship. Guitars and portable sound systems played the young man's favorite music, groupings of candles and flowers were renewed. Two young artists had drawn colorful messages with chalk on the sidewalk—to be seen from heaven?

I wondered how long this unusually long vigil would continue. Then one day Laguna Niguel maintenance trucks showed up in full force with an Orange County Sheriff's car. The sidewalk was blasted with high-pressure hoses. Orange caution tape cordoned off the area. Clearly the city officials were saying that the vigil was over. But you can't cordon off the human spirit. Even after several weeks I would still see one or two young people standing there, praying, singing, and crying.

Mary Margaret Hart Memorial, 2011. Author's collection.

I dip the asperges wand into the holy water bucket, then lift the wand and flick the sacred liquid left and right as the procession winds through the streets of the Logan Barrio in Santa Ana, California. Holy drops fall on invisible seeds of Grace. A cloud of sweet incense enfolds me, the thurible swinging side to side right behind me. Behind the thurifer, Father Ed Becker, the pastor of St. Joseph's Roman Catholic Church, holds a heavy gold monstrance, bearing the sacred host of the Body of Christ. It is Palm Sunday afternoon and this is the twentieth annual Blessing of the Streets.

About twenty years ago, an altar boy from St. Joseph's lay dying at the curb, across the street from the church, shot by local gangsters. The deadly pop-pop-pop sound was a daily occurrence in our area. Something had to be done. My Episcopal parish, Church of the Messiah, two blocks west of St. Joseph's, began to work with the local police department and St. Joseph's in developing community-based policing. My good friend, Father Christopher Smith, then pastor at St. Joseph's, initiated this Blessing of the Streets as a way for local churches to witness to our neighbors that Jesus is here in the streets and we are here as peacemakers. Again Jesus said, "Peace be with you. As the Father has sent me, I am sending you" (John 20:21).

Father Ed places the monstrance upon a small altar set up at the corner of French Street and 15th Street. On top of the altar is a large collage of photos of a young man who was murdered at this spot just three months before. His bright smiling face draws the prayerful attention of the five hundred mostly Latino and Polynesian marchers. Flowers and a small image of Our Lady of Guadalupe frame the photo of the young man. Father Ed disappears behind an apartment stairway and gently brings forward the tearful mother of the boy. We kneel before the Blessed Sacrament, singing:

> Bendito, bendito,
> Bendito sea Dios.
> > Los Angeles cantan y alaban a Dios.

What does all this mean?

As you drive on Highway 395 with Adelanto and Mojave to the south and Bridgeport to the north, you will pass many roadside shrines to victims of auto accidents. These shrines will be clustered along the deadliest section of the highway, between Olancha and Adelanto. The most lethal section north of Adelanto is called "Blood Highway." It has permanent bold double-yellow lines and signs posted: *No Passing Permitted*. Nonetheless, I have seen many a crazy driver in a large SUV pull out from behind a line of slower cars and pass. I have seen many near head-on collisions, the car coming in the opposite direction pulling to the side in a dangerous game of chicken.

Every week, the *Inyo Register*, newspaper for the Owens Valley, describes a grievous or fatal accident. It is a common tale: the driver falls asleep for a few seconds, the car drifts to the right, the driver panics, pulls the car to the left; either the car flips over several times, heading out into the desert, or drifts across the yellow line to hit another car head-on. Taking rest breaks is vital to safe driving, but the skiers going to Mammoth and other long-distance drivers become fatigued and terrible things happen.

There is a paradox here. I am driving through this spirit-soaked landscape, the result of volcanic eruptions, earthquakes and glacier melt. It is dramatic, majestic, glorious, and now, apart from the roadway, very quiet. On the road, inattentive to the power of their surroundings, people are fooling around with CD players, texting, and calling their friends. And in this rushing through the beautiful quiet, people die in grisly accidents.

One November morning I am driving north on 395 past the Haiwee Reservoir, south of Olancha. A red and black volcanic reef fills the prehistoric landscape to the east. Cottonwood trees flutter in the wind with last remnants of leaves. Winter is coming. A Christian cross appears suddenly on the right—you have to know the general location in order to find it. Written on the cross beam of this holy marker is *Margaret Mary Hart*. I see a cluster of sunflowers, roses in a case, some votive candles, and a picture of Margaret. She is smiling back at me through faded blue eyes. The cross is telling me, "This spot marks Margaret's doorway into heaven." There is a poem written by her niece, Danielle Edwards:

How am I supposed to live without you?

Your time here was not done.

You were the one I would go and talk to.

My life has just begun.

My heart aches because you're not here.

And never will be again.

But at least you felt no pain.The day before, I saw you

I didn't say goodbye.

The Night I would be without you

All I can do is cry.

I know this is God's plan.

I just can't understand.

I know he took you home.

I do not know why,

How can I be without you?

How can I say

Goodbye?

Cold wind rustles papers and flowers. The cross bends in resistance, marking a deadly automobile accident of several years ago. Recent offerings tell me that family and friends continue to visit. Why do they come here?

In the November 6, 2005, issue of the Barstow *Desert Dispatch*, Victorville family therapist Dr. Jim Shirley speaks of how families need to remember their loved ones: "It's a feeling of contact. Some people actively suppress memories so they won't be in grief. In some cases having a road-side memorial is a positive expression of grief. As long as those grieving move through the different stages of letting go. In some cases some people get stuck with the feeling and it becomes a problem."

Kelly Moon's daughter was killed in another auto accident on Mariposa Road, Hesperia. As any parent who has lost a child, Kelly thinks about her daughter every day. When the longing is especially hurtful, she doesn't go to the cemetery. She feels closest to her daughter when she visits the faded white memorial on Mariposa Road.

Before Olancha, a little further north on 395, yet another roadside memorial appears and a highway sign marks this section of the road in honor of California Highway Patrol officer Paul Pino. He had stopped an eighteen-wheeler truck and was sitting in his car talking on the radio to dispatch, when an inattentive SUV driver rammed Pino's patrol car into the truck, killing him. Marking that spot is another cross, candles, a teddy bear, three American flags, and a police jacket.

These memorials are telling you to slow down—I mean more than how fast you are driving, I mean how fast you are *living*. If you are following this guidebook, charting your next destination, perhaps trying to do too much today, these roadside memorials cry out to you: *Slow down your life and slow down your mind!*

Do it. Actually pull over for a moment, step out of your car into the desert sand. Walk over to this cross. *Remember me*. Remember that I also once lived, had a day of anticipation and plans, before my life suddenly ended. Remember me and my family. Pray for me. Today is one day. This hour is one hour. This minute is one minute. The breath you are breathing is one breath. Treasure this present moment, the gift of life you have right now. Consciously slow down your mind in the frantic movement between the past and the future. Stand here with me. Open your senses to all that surrounds you: the smell of sagebrush and juniper, the sound of wind and birds and, yes, cars and trucks speeding by. The warmth of the desert sun penetrates your body. You taste of the dry, cold morning air. The morning light coming out of Death Valley and illuminating Olancha Peak in the Sierra gently washes over you. And the memorials are saying, "You are alive and this is holy ground because I am remembered here and I am a precious child of God. As you remember me, I will pray you through the miles ahead."

During the great migration of Conestoga wagons in the early 1850s, from St. Joseph, Missouri, over the Sierra Nevada to Sacramento, thousands of pioneers pressed through vast prairies and endless dry deserts, possessed by dreams of gold. Accidents, disease, and violence claimed the lives of many. They were buried right there on the California Trail. And cowboys moving vast herds of cattle north out of Texas on the Chisholm Trail also died and were buried on the road. When civilization reached these parts, cemeteries were created with memorials of carved angels and heartfelt inscriptions.

Then some cemeteries became perhaps too civilized. When I visit my mother's grave at the Mountain View Cemetery in Altadena, I have a hard time finding her resting place. It takes me about twenty minutes to triangulate reference points: a wall, a pine tree, then walk down rows of similar marble plates imbedded in the grass, to find my mother's name. Only then can I kneel to clear the crabgrass off the marker and the dirt out of the inscription.However, the significant increase in roadside memorials, such as you will see on Highway 395, suggest our culture is going through a change in the way we remember our dead. We are not content with the anonymous and the insipid; today we want the personal and the particular. Set against the great desert, these shrines, with their offerings of flowers and memorabilia, tell me that Paul Pino and Margaret Mary Hart and Kelly Moon's daughter were unique and special people.

These roadside memorials are not a new phenomenon. Centuries of history are behind them. They are certainly part of our Hispanic California heritage. After Mass had been celebrated for the deceased, the funeral procession would move from the church and the coffin-bearers would stop to rest on the way to the graveyard. Each point of rest was a *descanso* and a small cross would be placed to mark the spot. As years passed, these *descansos* would be decorated on holidays with flowers and symbolic tokens in remembrance.

Today that same spirituality continues in the roadside memorials. But they also say something else to us as we hammer onward with cruise control set at eighty: this is a dangerous place to drive.

I say "we" advisedly.

July 20, 1964 was another magnificent California beach day. My girlfriend and I were driving to Santa Barbara on Highway 101. A blind curve. Stopped cars. Squealing brakes. My Chevrolet Tempest spun into the center divider. Cars coming from the opposite direction hit us and whirled us around and around. I was not wearing a seatbelt. An ice chest in the back seat crashed forward, hitting me. Amazingly, I was not knocked out, but a bloody gash opened in my head. Amazingly, my girlfriend and I were not killed or seriously injured. Now, every time I drive north on Highway 101 and pass the old road beside Emma Wood State Beach, I remember that day and the gift of life and years that followed.

The roadside memorials call out: *Remember me.* It is a common theme of spiritualties all over the world. Southern California must be among the most religiously diverse regions on Earth. For example, while the various forms of Buddhism are dispersed throughout the East, all forms of Buddhism can be found in Southern California: Vietnamese, Tibetan, Chinese. Then Sunni mosques, Shiite mosques, Jewish temples, and Sikh temples are sandwiched between Christian churches and Hindu temples. I can imagine driving 395 in the future and seeing not only crosses marking roadside memorials; there will be the Star of David or the Crescent of Islam or a Buddhist Bodhisattva.

All the religions of the world remember the dead. In venerating the dead there is a belief that our deceased continue to be connected to the living and can communicate blessings or warnings for the future. African immigrants to our country bring with them a belief in the ancestors living on. If someone of African heritage is buried here, his or her family may continue to show respect and to honor them by leaving flowers, pouring a libation of wine or whisky on the ground, and leaving a food offering. Remembering the ancestors and attending to them can bring blessings. Forgetting them can bring trouble such as sickness.

Asian immigrants to America see a core value in paying filial honor to their parents and other elders. Taoist traditions include burning paper facsimiles of things needed in the afterlife: a house, a Lexus, and an iPhone. The Other Side mirrors this world, and there the inhabitants need food, clothing, shelter, and transportation. In the Asian communities of Orange County, Los Angeles, and San Francisco, street vendors sell these picture offerings to be burned at home or at the temple and so transferred to the beloved dead. I remember preparing for a funeral at Fairhaven Cemetery in Santa Ana. The family had not yet arrived. As I waited beside my car, dressed in a priest's cassock and clutching the holy water, I looked at the gravesite at the curb next to me. Right in front of me on the green grass was a fresh dim sum bun, a Chinese newspaper, and a Starbuck's specialty tea. All of this surrounded a grave plaque inscribed in Chinese. This family was expressing their devotion to a beloved patriarch.

Vietnamese parishioners in my congregation tell me that before or after the Christian ritual of burial a family will frequently perform the old Taoist rituals as well, so that the soul will not become a hungry ghost.

At the heart of the Christian tradition of remembering the dead is the Communion of Saints. I remember that my own mother, Linnea Victoria Marguerita Karelius, died on Easter Day morning, 1989. Through several months of dumb grief, I was unable to pray about it, until one night, in praying the Examen of Conscience, I began to imagine my mother in heaven, with Jesus and Mary and the saints. She had been sick and suffering for years. Now I could sense her prayers for me, on this side of life. Christians believe that this bond of love is eternal. As Easter Day was Jesus' conquest of the enemy, Death, so we can live in hope in a continuing connection with those who have died and who now pray us through our daily lives.

As we drive through the hauntingly beautiful landscape of the Owens Valley, we pass special places, "thin places" as the Celtic mystics would say, where connection and communion with the Holy is especially possible. Here, the barrier between one world and the other is permeable. This book is a guide to some of those places. I believe that a roadside memorial can be for you and me such a place. In this vast, expansive space there are points that have holy meaning.

My friend Walter Brueggemann writes about the spiritual meaning of places that have a sacred story:

> Place is a space which has historical meanings, where some things have happened which are now remembered and which provide continuity and identity across generations. Place is space in which important words have been spoken which have established identity, defined vocation and envisioned destiny. Place is space in which vows have been exchanged, promises have been made, and demands have been issued. Place is indeed a protest against an uncompromising pursuit of space. It is a declaration that our humanness cannot be found in escape, detachment, absence of commitment, and undefined freedom. . . . Whereas a pursuit of space may be a flight from history, a yearning for a place is a decision to enter history with an identifiable people in an identifiable pilgrimage.[3]

3. Brueggemann, *Land*, 4.

The sense of self being attached to, involved in, and imbued with a place on Earth may begin with being watchful for these memorials (while driving carefully and responsibly!). At the site you can look for a name and other signs of the life that is remembered here—a mother, a child, a family. Here, in an instant, a life ended because of a traffic accident. You can sense a family's longing to remember a beloved one. You can also gain a renewed sense of the gift of your own life, how all of us go through each present moment living in Amazing Grace.

How can I live most gratefully and responsibly with the ongoing gifts of this chain of present moments?

2

Compassionate Mother of the Desert

Mother of Love and Compassion,

Bestow your wisdom upon me.

Help me see humanity through your eyes.

Help me master the love and compassion

that you hold near your heart of God.

Help me shine like a beacon in the night and

see my reflection in your tear of love.

Kuan Yin, I thank you for your tireless love

and your patience and hope for humanity.

Shanti, Shanti, Shanti, Amen.

—GODDESS AND BODHISATTVA QUAN YIN[1]

HOW THE LANDSCAPE HAS changed! It is 6:30 on a Wednesday morning. I am driving toward the Owens Valley via Highway 91 through Corona and north on Interstate 15. Only a few years ago I would be passing through Dutch dairy country, with thousands of black and white Holsteins packed together in feeding pens in view of the highway. The smell in summer heat could take your breath away! Today dense suburban housing covers the land as far as I can see. I will bet the houses now have verdant lawns and gardens, given what they replaced!

1. Quoted from http://quanyinhealings.blogspot.com/2009/01/quan-yin-blessing-mother-of-love-and.html.

As the freeway draws me closer to the mountains, dense morning fog enfolds ghostly shapes of the old vineyards of Cucamonga and Guasti. More new housing with instant avenues of palm trees crowd the gnarled, enfeebled vines.

I begin the climb over Cajon Pass. Snaking lines of eighteen-wheelers wind up the steep grade. Passenger cars whizz by, headed to Las Vegas. At the summit, the blanketing fog retreats and brilliant desert sun fills the morning light. The turnoff to Highway 395 leading toward the Owens Valley comes quickly, so you have to be watching out for it.

Previously I could anticipate endless desert landscape filled with creosote bushes and sagebrush. But yet again, this ancient land has been scraped away for closely packed new suburbs. How strange to see compactly planned neighborhoods with high walls around them, still surrounded by remnants of the desert! This is Adelanto. Some of my parishioners in Santa Ana moved here to find a cheaper home and get away from the lures and pressures of gang life that their children had to negotiate. But the gangs moved here too. We pass through Adelanto, and at last unspoiled desert landscape beckons. Soon we are back into the sagebrush ocean spilling out for miles east and west. No fences here. Wide open spaces. Just as I prepare for a long drive through vast landscape, *she* appears in the sagebrush as a great surprise.

I quickly pull off the road. What *is* that? The early morning light reflects pink and orange off a huge white statue. I drive through an open gate toward the shape. As I draw closer, the figure grows more recognizable. This has to be the largest image I have seen of the Asian Buddhist bodhisattva Kuan Yin, the Compassionate Mother. Here in the middle of nowhere. What is going on? I park and walk closer. A stone walkway leads past a mobile home to the twenty-five-foot statue of Kuan Yin expressed in traditional sculpture.

She is cloaked in white, the color of purity. Sometimes she is holding a rosary of Buddhist prayer beads. She is also shown with a book of the Lotus Sutra. I have seen her image holding a child, which is a reminder that she is the patron saint of barren women. She could also be standing on a dragon, a Taoist image of alchemy and eternal life. Here in this desert she holds a vase, symbolizing her pouring compassion into the world.

Two women stand in front of the image, one holding a stick of incense between her hands in reverence. They are chanting Kuan Yin's mantra: *Om mani padme hum*, "Hail the jewel in the lotus!" They are sharing *darshan*, the Hindu-Buddhist state of prayer in which one sees and is seen by the Divine. By doing darshan properly a devotee develops affection for the deity and the deity develops affection for the devotee. As I gaze at the women, deep in their devotional chanting, I see a love affair with the divine.

One of the women shares with me that she heard about the healing power of Kuan Yin and that here in the desert her powers were stronger than anywhere else. There are stories that Kuan Yin would often emanate a white light and people would see a rainbow covering her head. The woman who spoke to me had lifelong arthritis in her shoulders and arms. Her frequent visits to the shrine have healed her so that the pain has almost disappeared. She picks up a bottle of holy water from the altar nearby; its Chi potency has increased through Kuan Yin's blessing.

A short, stout man wrapped in monk's robes walks toward us. Monk Thich Dang "Tom" Phap was a captain in the South Vietnamese Army for ten years from 1965. After capture by the Viet Cong, he spent two years in prison. He has seen much suffering and death. After his release, he was able to come to America. He had a dream one night in which the Buddha called him to be a monk. And here he is. He says, "When we began to clear away the sagebrush for Kuan Yin, there were many snakes. I talked with them compassionately and told them what we were doing here and to please not bother us, and they have stayed away."

It was the Buddha who gave Thich Dang Phap the vision of a meditation center in the middle of the desert. He is a monk with an incredible gift for generating enthusiasm and for raising money. Every time I drive by the center, there is new activity; the gardens have been expanded, new statues have been imported from Vietnam. (I later learn that these statues come from the village of Non Nuoc, the center of stone carving in Da Nang.) In 2011, a magnificent new Buddhist temple was built as the centerpiece of devotion. Every weekend, hundreds of Asian Buddhists make the trip from Orange County and as a far away as San Francisco to this place of potent healing by the compassionate Mother of the Desert. If you make the journey and don't know much about Buddhism, the following sketch may help.

Kuan Yin Bodhisattva, 2008. Author's collection.

The Great Spiritual Awakening in the United States of the 1960s shares similarities with the birth of Buddhism in the sixth century BCE. In India of that time, the general religious culture, Vedic Hinduism, had evolved into a complex system of rituals, requiring expensive and time-consuming efforts by many priests. And so, the religious traditions of India became disconnected from popular piety. People moved away from the religious centers to the forests. Under the guidance of a guru and varieties of yoga, people experienced personal enlightenment through union of their soul/atman with Brahman/God. They experienced what the Greek New Testament terms *metanoia,* a life-changing encounter with the Holy. The sermons and instruction of these gurus inspired another set of sacred scripture, the *Upanishads.*

In the United States of the later 1960s, people turned to the Eastern practice of meditation to gain life-changing experiences. Up to that time, the word "spirituality" was not in common conversation. It was a word that was identified with monasteries and monks such as Thomas Merton. Traditional Christianity, at the core of American culture, was in crisis. People were seeking personal communion with the Holy.

Siddhartha Gautama, who became the Buddha, was born into a cultural cusp of emerging spirituality in India. Raised in a sheltered royal enclave, where his every desire was catered to, he became aware of an emptiness in his heart and he escaped from the walled palace into the world, where he saw for the first time a sick person, an aged person, and a corpse. He also saw an ascetic, a naked *shramana,* who wandered about, owning nothing. Siddhartha tried many paths toward enlightenment. He himself became the most austere of ascetics, but still he found no peace. Giving up that effort, he returned to what was familiar to him, perhaps a form of Raja Yoga. Meditating under a tree in the light of the full moon of May, his mind became still. As he fell into the deepest levels of consciousness, he remembered all the details of his past lives, the endless stream of existences. He saw the lives of all other creatures, their struggles, triumphs, and failures. He could perceive the rhythm of their lives: birth, death, birth, death, the endless pulse of *samsara.*

In deep, focused meditation, Siddhartha could see the pattern of this ceaseless flux of change/samsara. Those whose lives were based on compassion and generosity were reborn into a higher state. Those who gave into greed and violence and hatred were reborn into a lower state of suffering. Like an Indian doctor, he diagnosed the core spiritual problem of existence: birth and death followed from craving and attachment. With the ending of craving, the cycle of birth and death and suffering ceased. Siddhartha had become the *Buddha,* the Awakened One. He was no longer subject to samsara.

If the Four Noble Truths became the diagnosis, then the Fourth Truth is the pharmaceutical prescription: the Eightfold Path. It is a life process of waking up to our true nature. The key vehicle for waking up is meditation.

Our hearts, filled with desire and anxiety, move back and forth between the past, which cannot be reactivated, and the future, which by definition is that which is not yet. The only thing that is *real* is the present moment, this present breath. Meditation is the guide to waking up to what is real, and seeing how we have created a world of false permanence, in which we believe we are self-sufficient entities.

At the beginnings of the movement that became Buddhism, only the full-time monk could be dedicated to this Way. In modern terms, it is really a self-help method. No gods, dogma, or rituals can help you. This oldest form of Buddhism, Theravada Buddhism, was lived in monastic community known as the *sangha*.

As Buddhism traveled into other lands, it developed flexibility. Not all of the Buddha's teachings (*dharma*) were written down. Some were given only to select disciples in secret. This allowed for interpretation. In addition, the belief arose that the Buddha was not only a man, but also a supernatural being. There were other beings, bodhisattvas, who had achieved release from the cycle of life and death, but who out of compassion remained in this world to help all of us over the river of life.

This is a central tenet of Mahayana Buddhism, as expressed at the temple just outside Adelanto. And here is the Compassionate Mother, Kuan Yin. Just as the Christian reverence for the Virgin Mary may be (in part) a popular reaction to patriarchal control of the church, Kuan Yin is more popular than any of the male bodhisattvas. She is honored in a great many Asian homes as the most powerful spiritual being.

Author with Master Tom and brother monk, 2013. Author's collection.

I asked one of the women before the statue how Buddhism helped her become more compassionate. She said that wisdom and compassion go together. They are like two eyes that help us see reality and to wake up to our true nature. Compassion/*karuna* is an active spirituality whereby we are willing to bear the pain and suffering of others. We are to selflessly respond to alleviate any suffering that we encounter. Meditation does soften our hearts, but we need the help of Kuan Yin to do this great work.

A pamphlet at the center quotes from the Dali Lama's *Essence of the Heart Sutra*:

> According to Buddhism, compassion is an aspiration, a state of mind, wanting others to be free from suffering. It's not passive—it's not empathy alone—but rather an empathetic altruism that actively strives to free others from suffering. Genuine compassion must have both wisdom and loving-kindness. That is to say, one must understand the nature of the suffering from which we wish to free others (this is wisdom), and one must experience deep intimacy and empathy with other sentient beings (this is loving-kindness).[2]

I visit the Center each time I travel into the Owens Valley. I now have these new spiritual friends, the two sisters and Monk Tom. And I now have Kuan Yin's blessing as I travel the most dangerous part of Highway 395, which is between Adelanto and the junction with Highway 14.

---

2. Bstan-'dzin-rgya-mtsho, *Essence of the Heart Sutra*, ch. 5, ¶2.

3

Religious Differences and Mutual Transformation

The longest journey is the journey inward.

—Dag Hammarskjold[1]

Wisdom cannot be imparted. Wisdom that a wise man attempts to impart always sounds like foolishness to someone else. . . . Knowledge can be communicated, but not wisdom. One can find it, live it, do wonders through it, but one cannot communicate and teach it.

—Hermann Hesse[2]

There is a price to be paid for any genuine pluralism. It is that there is no longer a center. There are many. The others must become genuine others to us—not projections of our fears and desires.

—David Tracy[3]

THE FIRST CLASS OF a new semester is always magical for me: a clean slate, tabula rasa, a new beginning. As I gaze at the students filling the large lecture hall in the Science & Math building at Saddleback Community College,

1. Hammarskjöld, *Markings*, 58.
2. Hesse, *Siddhartha*, 142.
3. Tracy, *On Naming the Present*, 4.

Mission Viejo, my stomach rumbles with nervous energy: my fortieth year of teaching, but it seems like I am just beginning.

Years ago, the makeup of the class was mostly Anglo and Christian, but over the last few years all the world's religions have arrived in this classroom. Since the 1970s, Orange County has become a center of immigration for people from South Asia and East Asia. Students from Pakistan, India, Viet Nam, Cambodia, and China are now a common sight at Saddleback College.

World Religions, Philosophy 10. A three-hour lecture on Thursday nights. I begin the first lecture with an invitation that is a warning and a caveat: "The subject we will be studying together is the most important subject you will explore in college and it will change your life. You and I will be different persons seventeen weeks from now."

I wonder if they believe me?

I push on. "For some of you our work together will involve a significant personal challenge. For those of you who come from a religious tradition in which you see your beliefs as *the* true religion, explorations of other religions may cause you apprehension. 'Will this study weaken my own faith? Will reading about these "pagan" religions expose me to temptation and a dilution of my commitment to my God?' Those of you who are agnostic, atheist, or are reactive to religion and spirituality have another challenge. You may have had a negative personal experience with religion or you may hold the intellectual position that religion and spirituality are for neurotic people. This may blind and inhibit you from seeing the treasure and gifts in the various spiritualities we will study."

I push on further. I share with my students that I have been a philosophy professor at Saddleback Community College since 1973 and a full-time parish priest in Orange County since 1970. The part about my being a priest will push buttons. Some students who do not believe that the teacher-priest combination can provide an objective learning experience will withdraw from the class at the first break. I counter this reaction by reminding my students that as a state-licensed instructor I am not permitted to proselytize my own religion, though I am allowed to teach the subject with a deep passion, which I do.

With this out of the way, I begin by reflecting on Dr. Diana Eck's seminal book, *Encountering God: A Spiritual Journey from Bozeman to Banaras*.

She presents three positions from which we can engage the world religions other than our own. Firstly, the Exclusivist: my religion is the only revealed truth. I may study other religions as a subject, but my religion is the one, true path. Secondly, the Inclusivist: my religion is one among many, each of varying validity. Thirdly, the Pluralist: there are many voices that speak; none has a monopoly of truth; each is valid in context.

Dr. Eck asks us: How are we to live with one another in a climate of mutuality and understanding? She develops the orientation of pluralism for us. Be careful here as you read this: this is not a process that will transform a believer into an inclusivist. Below is a summary of Dr. Eck's insights about pluralism. Her words are in quotes[4] and my commentary follows. The matter is complicated, but she is a good guide.

"Pluralism is not the sheer fact of plurality alone, but is active engagement with plurality. I can observe and celebrate diversity, but I have to *participate* in pluralism." I live in Southern California, perhaps the most religiously diverse region in America. I can be a cultural tourist, visiting houses of worship and colorful religious festivals. Pluralism requires a genuine desire to understand these different traditions and participate in dialogue with members of their religious communities.

"Pluralism means more than toleration, it also seeks understanding." I can be tolerant of our Shia Muslim neighbor. After another long summer day of Ramadan fasting, her extended family fills the parking spaces in front of her house. The night air carries aromas of roasting meat and garlic and sounds of fervent singing. Pluralism urges me to speak with her about what this holy season means to her and her immigrant family, living far from their homeland.

"Pluralism is not simply relativism, but assumes real commitment." Living in this richly diverse cultural garden of Southern California, I encounter people who are students of world religions. They collect books and CD lectures on the subject, but they are perpetual shoppers. Pluralism requires that I am rooted in a religious community, warts and all, and understand (at least to some extent) the beliefs of my own tradition.

"Pluralism is not syncretism, but is based in complete respect for differences." The goal of pluralism is not to create a universal spiritual community that ignores the sharp differences between religions, which have, historically, influenced many conflicts between nations.

One of the syllabus requirements for my students in our world religion classes is to visit a house of worship that is not of their own tradition. I urge the student to consider visiting a religious tradition for which they have a

---

4. Quotations are from Eck, *Encountering God*, 191–99.

visceral negative feeling, even though they may have had little contact with that religion. As they prepare for this class assignment, each student should research the ritual or prayer event they will attend, so that it will not all be a mystery. I encourage the students to call ahead and make contact with someone. Hopefully that contact will meet them on the student's arrival and perhaps guide them through the experience. I want each student to participate as best they can in the prayers and rituals, rather than sitting on the sidelines taking notes. Usually the student engages the host contact in some reflective dialogue after the experience. Differences will be noted. I ask each student to consider their prejudgments about that religion before their visit and consider, a day or so later, how the experience has changed them.

"Pluralism is based on interreligious dialogue. The language of dialogue is the two-way language of real encounter. Mutual transformation goes beyond simply understanding each other, to the point that the participants gain new levels of self-understanding."

Now I remind my students that among their family and friends and acquaintances there is at least one person who is from a different religion than theirs. In this class, I will help the student understand the basic beliefs, vocabulary, similarities, and differences among the world religions. These will be the tools they will use in the work of mutual transformation. We will model dialogue in the class to invite the students to go back into their worlds to seek opportunities to talk, share, listen, and learn in the exchange with others.

Nevertheless, here is the challenge: students must have a sense of what they believe. And they must be able to articulate those beliefs insofar as language permits. If they are Christian, they may find that the Muslim, Jew, or Buddhist may know more about Christianity than they do. Pluralism means I come from the integrity of my deeply held spiritual beliefs and values and I enter into dialogue with another. We have to watch ourselves here to make sure that dialogue does not become debate. If, tacitly, you begin with the goal of changing the other person, the process will be stunted. But if you are open to listening, and have the courage to express what you believe, both you and your interlocutor will be transformed.

You can see that one of my key goals in teaching is peacemaking. If the main cause of world conflicts has been religious differences, I can help my students understand the Other, know themselves, and take a hard look at their own prejudice and ignorance about the Other.

I am a committed Christian. The Spiritual Exercises of St. Ignatius Loyola have really helped me to seek communion with the Jesus expressed in the Gospels, to invite his presence and guidance throughout my daily life. I know that my True Self is found in Jesus. For me, Jesus is the Way, the Truth, and the Life. I also see treasures in the other religious traditions, which help me to be a better Christian. William Johnston, SJ, in his book *Silent Music*, tells us how his lifelong study of Zen meditation has helped him to pray to Jesus. And Thomas Merton revealed in his study of Taoism and Zen Buddhism how this helped him to be a more faithful Christian disciple and monk. In his *The Way of Chuang Tzu*, Merton writes:

> I have been a Christian monk for nearly twenty-five years, and inevitably one comes in time to see life from a viewpoint that has been common in solitaries and recluses in all ages and in all cultures.[5]

And a little later he adds,

> I think I may be pardoned for consorting with a Chinese recluse who shares the climate and peace of my own kind of solitude, and who is my own kind of person.[6]

And now I share with my students that it is *mysticism* that connects the various world spiritualities. And it is the desert that is a common place for mystical encounters with the Holy. There are several pathways in the desert. They are often rugged, they often cross each other, they converge. Every day we encounter persons from other religions. Every day we have the opportunity for dialogue and mutual transformation. The desert gives us the spiritual ballast for this great work.

In his blog post titled "The Major Points of Convergence within the Great Spiritual Traditions," the contemporary Catholic writer Father Ron Rolheiser speaks very clearly about the things that are common to the great religious traditions. I quote:

- "In all of them the aim of the spiritual quest is the same: union with God and union with everyone and everything else."

5. Merton, *Way of Chuang Tzu*, 10.
6. Ibid., 11.

- "The path to union is understood as coming through compassion."
- "The route to compassion and union with God is paradoxical, requiring that somehow we have to lose ourselves to find ourselves."
- "Spiritual progress requires hard discipline and some painful renunciations."
- "The spiritual quest is a life-long journey with no short-cuts."
- "Religious fervor and dark nights of the soul both have an important role within the spiritual journey."
- "Extraordinary phenomena within the spiritual journey . . . are all downplayed."
- "While we are on the spiritual path, we will meet great temptations and powerful demons and these need to be recognized and taken seriously."
- "The spiritual journey will always partly be a mystery."
- "The road is narrow and hard."

I imagine this: There is a large dark room (similar to my lecture hall). Several people spend a long time in deep meditation in the darkness, unaware that there are others there in the same space. One is Thomas Merton, the Christian monk; another is the Dali Lama; others are a Sufi Muslim, a Hassidic Jew, a Hindu Sadhu, a Paiute Shaman, and people of other religions. After a very long time, the lights go on. The people stand up and walk towards the center of the room. There are no words. They gaze into each other's eyes and see that they have been in the same spiritual space in their encounters with the Holy.

4

Passing Parade at Little Lake

Do they not observe the birds above them, spreading their wings and folding them in? None can uphold them except (Allah) Most Gracious: Truly it is He that watches over all things.

—QURAN 67:19[1]

WINTER RAINS HAVE BEEN abundant in the Owens Valley this year and heavy snow covers the Sierra. Highway 395, beyond the intersection with Highway 14, winds through huge volcanic reefs towards a narrow notch between mountain ranges. It is not hard to imagine the flow of the lava from the active volcanoes twenty-five thousand years ago.

Once you pass through the notch, you arrive at Little Lake. On your right is a blue-green shallow lake, an oasis in this desert land. Thousands of waterfowl and shorebirds visit this lake during autumn and spring. Your journey will take you to a breathtaking overlook and a wonderful place for contemplation.

Continue north on Highway 395 for twenty-four miles from the intersection of Highway 14. As you pass Little Lake, clearly ahead of you is an old volcano: Red Cinder Cone. Head directly for this natural feature. Just before it, you will see the sign for Cinder Road and signs for Fossil Falls and Little Lake. The Overlook is 4.9 miles from the highway. Travel past Fossil Falls about two miles to Power Line Road. Turn south (right) on Power Line Road and follow the signs to Little Lake Overlook for 2.75 miles. Turn west (right) to the entrance.

---

1. Yusuf Ali, trans., *Meaning of the Holy Qur'an*, 1501.

The broken, pitted road winds through open desert and onto a volcanic reef. In the spring there should be wild flowers. As you park your car, you will see what remains of Little Lake before you; there are only hints that once civilization made a stab at establishing itself here. Sagebrush and creosote have reclaimed their space and the rail bed fades into the landscape, but here there are some benches on which to sit and contemplate the magnificent view. Ahead of you, to the west, is the Sierra Nevada. You can see the highway. Notice the other side of the highway and a road branching off to the side. This is where for a hundred years Little Lake stood. There was a stone-walled hotel and gas station, and the Southern Pacific Railroad had a branch line that ran through here from Mojave to Lone Pine. Tourists in the 1920s would travel up from Los Angeles, stay at the hotel, and fish and swim in the lake. The hotel burned in 2000 and the rails from the railroad were taken up five years later. Almost nothing remains of Little Lake, except for some quaintly painted advertisements on flat rocks nearby.

It is early summer, 1978. My wife, Jan, and our little daughter are traveling north to camp at Bridgeport. It is the kind of clear, scorching day that drives into your sinuses like a hot poker. After three hours on the road our stomachs are rumbling for breakfast—and there it is, tucked between the volcanic reefs, the busy Little Lake hotel. Cars are parked every which way, and the gas station is busy with water pump repairs. I open the heavy steel-frame wooden door and enter the restaurant: high, cobwebbed ceilings, open pine-beam supports, three-foot-thick walls of basalt; the temperature drops about twenty degrees. We find the only empty table, which is made of a hand-hewn slab of pine, the initials of previous diners carved into it. As we wait to be served, the water glasses suddenly start to shake. Earthquake? A diesel locomotive blasts its distant warning; the closer it comes, the more we vibrate. The Southern Pacific freight passes up the steep grade on its way to Lone Pine. Boxcars swish by, then silence.

View of Little Lake and Red Cinder Cone, 2009. Author's collection.

As you walk to the edge of the reef, watch out for the sharp volcanic rocks. Between the highway and the lake is a site much older than the vanished settlement of Little Lake. A Pinto or Lake Mojave Native American village existed here more than six thousand years ago on the south end of the lake. This was the Koso Panamint winter village of Pagunda. Around this site are plenty of examples of rock art and petroglyphs. In 1947, Willy Stahl, an amateur archaeologist, discovered evidence of this early native settlement in a small cave near the lake. These were Pinto people who made obsidian projectile points in a distinctive style. The whole site and its petroglyphs are protected behind barriers and are located on private property, but there are frequent tours in the spring and fall conducted through the Maturango Museum in Ridgecrest.

I sit on the bench on Little Lake Overlook and I watch this history. I imagine a rapid time-lapse movie: smoke rises from the cone-shaped reed shelters of the native village. Reed boats float on the lake, men are fishing, women are grinding pine nuts on flat rocks, and children are running on the lakeshore, splashing water. The film advances. A bright red Wells Fargo stagecoach pulled by six proud, black horses rides through a cloud of dust. The coach stops at a rude wooden stage station beside the lake. Impatient, gold-hungry miners heading to Cerro Gordo pace nervously as the horses are changed. In the next scene, the Pinto village is gone, and the stone hotel and railroad appear. Here comes a steam locomotive belching smoke to the sound of a shrill whistle. Then the dirt road going past the hotel becomes dotted with Model-T Fords. I can see some folk on the side of the road filling their steaming radiator. The film advances. The road is now paved. Eighteen-wheelers are carrying heavy loads and SUVs packed with skiers drive furiously north to Mammoth. A golden eagle darts past me towards a rock crevasse below, and a flock of white pelicans land on the lake.

In this ancient land, change is slow but constant. As I sit quietly on this bench, feeling the warmth of the sun and the caress of the dry wind scented with sagebrush, my racing mind has quieted. I focus on my breath, this present breath. I am anchored to this place and God's wondrous creation. The work, struggle, and ambitions of human life acted out before me in the scenes below are memories. This present moment is *real* in this present breath I am taking. The vast expanse of this desert space opens my heart to God's huge, compassionate love.

And now I remember the prayer of St. Francis, his "Canticle of the Sun," and offer it up to the Lord:

O most High, almighty, good Lord God,
to you belong praise, glory, honor, and all blessing!

Praised be my Lord God with all creatures;
and especially our brother the sun,
which brings us the day and the light;
fair is he, and shining with a very great splendor:
O Lord, he signifies you to us!

Praised be my Lord for our sister the moon,
and for the stars,
which God has set clear and lovely in heaven.

Praised be my Lord for our brother the wind,
and for air and cloud, calms and all weather,
by which you uphold in life all creatures.

Praised be my Lord for our sister water,
which is very serviceable to us,
and humble, and precious, and clean.

Praised be my Lord for brother fire,
through which you give us light in the darkness;
and he is bright, and pleasant, and very mighty, and strong.

Praised be my Lord for all those who pardon
one another for God's love's sake,
and who endure weakness and tribulation;
blessed are they who peaceably shall endure,
for you, O Most High, shall give them a crown!
. . .

Praised be my Lord for our sister,
the death of the body, from which no one escapes.
Woe to him who died in mortal sin!
Blessed are they who are found walking by your most holy will,
for the second death shall have no power to do them harm.

Praise you, and bless you the Lord,
and give thanks to God, and serve God with great humility.[2]

Sitting on this bench overlooking Little Lake, I am meditating on St. Francis' powerful text. This canticle is more than warm, romantic feelings for the natural world. I believe that Francis is singing that the living and non-living beings of creation are our brothers and sisters who reflect to us the face of the Holy One. Each created thing is a particular, specific revelation of this Holy One. For Christians, the core of this revelation is that Jesus of Nazareth came among us as a brother, a fellow creature. At Little Lake we encounter the cosmic fraternity of which Francis sings, in the birds who find refuge here. Francis was especially fond of birds; they were his special congregation and he would often preach to them.

2. Quoted from http://www.usccb.org/prayer-and-worship/prayers-and-devotions/prayers/prayers-to-care-for-creation.cfm.

And I realize that at this moment I have a have a front-row seat to Nature's grand runway! Especially during the northern and southern migrations, flocks of ducks, grebes, cormorants, and American white pelicans circle and glide in to land on the water. I have seen great blue herons poking into the water for fish on the shallow bank. And I remember a bald eagle swooping in from a high altitude on a cloudy day in December.

Watching birds is itself a restful meditation. Sit quietly and be still. Wait. When they come into sight, what do you first notice about those birds? What strikes you about color and behavior? Take a closer look with binoculars, noting color on parts of the body, wings, belly and head. There are local Sierra field guides to help you identify your visitors.

Be watchful and alert. At first, you may not see anything distinctive. If you look more carefully around Little Lake, on fences, rocks along the water, branches floating in the lake, you may see something move. Take the time to listen for the songs and sounds of the birds to help you locate and identify them. As you practice being attentive, you will be able to see that there is a multitude of wild birds coming and going from the lake.

Let me share an experience. Several years ago, I drove up Mazurka Canyon, east of the town of Independence in the Inyo Mountains. I parked and found a large flat rock to lay out lunch. I could enjoy the view of the valley from there and I sat for some time quietly watching and listening in the low brush. The monotonous brown-grey blur of the landscape began to take on a high-definition texture and I could see a small brilliant-blue bird. A Sierra bluebird! I had never seen one before. My eyes adjusted in my quiet contemplation and suddenly I could see dozens balancing on the brush. I was surrounded by brilliant dainty gems! I later learned that the Sierra bluebird lives in colonies in isolated places like this.

Little Lake has taught me about the transience of human experience—a basic Buddhist insight—and about how Nature gives of itself abundantly when we are still and quiet and allow our eyes to see.

On Highway 395, between Little Lake and Bridgeport, there are thirty-eight unique vista points on the Eastern Sierra Birding Trail. There is a free guide to these points that can be obtained at the Lone Pine Visitor Center. You can also visit the website at www.easternsierrabirdingtrail.org.

5

The Singing Tree

The cottonwood . . . is a tree particularly sacred to many Indian peoples in the West. Always chosen by the Sioux for use in the Sun Dance ceremony, this tree is regarded as holy because it can grow where most others cannot. Furthermore, the rustling of its leaves even in the slightest breeze is said to form a continuous prayer to Wakan-Tanka, the Great Spirit. There is a unity shared here by all those beings whose life is knit to the land and its ways . . . their lives were intertwined, connected at the Middle Place where the earth blossoms in shares of gold, blue, white and black—-the colors of the four corners, the colors of life's varied and changing seasons.

—BELDEN LANE[1]

Perhaps you have noticed that even in the very lightest breeze you can hear the voice of the cottonwood tree; this we understand is its prayer to the Great Spirit; for not only men, but all things and all beings pray to Him continually in differing ways.

—BLACK ELK[2]

MOTHER NATURE HAS TURNED on the furnace. A searing hot wind blows out of Death Valley into the Owens Valley. Driving north on Highway 395, I catch first sight of Owens Lake, now covered with the pink patina of tiny

1. Lane, *Landscapes of the Sacred*, 80.
2. Black Elk, *Sacred Pipe*, 75.

shrimp living in the caustic brine that blooms in the summer. This is not a good time to be traveling through the desert. 103 °F at one in the afternoon. I am heading for Carson City, Nevada, to another archaeology dig with the University of Nevada at Reno.

My body relaxes at first sight of the huge green trees lining the highway about three miles ahead at the historic stage stop of Olancha. There is a story that explains the straight lines of cottonwoods on each side of the highway. Back in 1870, a rancher used cut cottonwood branches to fence his land. Because of the high water table, the fence took root, and cottonwood trees were resurrected from the old branches *in situ*.

I have been enchanted by the cottonwood tree for years, and for years I did not really know why. I knew only that it was the tallest tree in the Owens Valley, that it provided extensive shade, and that the sound of the wind rustling the leaves captivated me. Something deep inside me felt a communion with this tree. Only recently did I learn about the extensive botanical and anthropological background of the Freemont cottonwood.

The air-conditioning in the Honda Pilot is working hard, but still the bone-dry heat assails me as though my head were wrapped in a sack of needles. The trees approach—lush, green, giant umbrellas. I arrive at my favorite rest stop, the Ranch House Café, parking next to a freight truck loaded with hay bales. The smell of cattle permeates the sultry day, drifting over from fenced pastures on the lakeside. My car is sheltered by the shade of an ancient cottonwood tree, broken and twisted and burned from repeated lighting strikes. Green branches persistently push toward the sun out of the old wood. Boots step on soft hot sand and I walk toward a cluster of cottonwoods, savoring the cool shade. And now the temperature drops markedly. This beats air-conditioning! A breeze catches the branches of the trees and I listen to my favorite sound in Nature: the rustling of the leaves of the cottonwood. However, this is not a good season for a contemplative walk.

I return to this same site in November. It is a different, beautiful world. My car is parked beside the same old gnarled tree, but now she is clothed in the shimmering gold of fall. I walk a dirt road away from the noise of 395 in the direction of the Sierra Nevada. The prominent, iconic image of Olancha Peak thrusts upward, the same image that appears on the label of Crystal Geyser water bottles produced out of Olancha Creek, a half-mile north. I sit on the battered corpse of an old cottonwood, sipping that water.

The pungent, sweet smell of mesquite wood burning in a fireplace drifts over from a cabin nearby. Now it is quiet and I can listen to the music of the wind caressing the cottonwoods. There is no sound like this. The Hopi of Arizona believe that the cottonwood is a sacred tree and that the rustling of the wind through the quaking leaves is the gods speaking to the people.

A branch hangs low and I can take a closer look at the phenomenon whence this magical sound emanates. The leaves are heart-shaped, with petioles equal to half the blade length, laterally compressed near the blade, and this shape causes the leaves to flutter in the wind. That is the word: *flutter*. Behold this wondrous tree! Ninety feet tall, golden yellow leaves fluttering and shimmering. Sit with me on this tree trunk by its living neighbors. Behold the hypnotic scene of dancing leaves and musical fluttering! God must be close to us now.

Perhaps the Hasidic Jewish mystic Martin Buber sat on a tree like this cottonwood when he was inspired to write his seminal book *I and Thou* (*Ich und Du*), published in 1923.

> I consider a tree. I can look on it as a picture: stiff column in a shock of light, or splash of green shot with the delicate blue and silver of the background. I can perceive it as movement: flowing veins on clinging, pressing pith, suck of the roots, breathing of the leaves, ceaseless commerce with earth and air—and the obscure growth itself.[3]

I can place it somewhere in the Linnaean system of botany: this cottonwood tree is *Populus fremontii*. In all of this intense observation, that tree remains an object, an *It*. Buber continues:

> It can, however, also come about, if I have both will and grace, that in considering the tree I become bound up in relation to it. The tree is now no longer *It*.[4]

Buber sits on the old tree trunk with you and me, taking in that entire old cottonwood. It is fully present to him here and now. He experiences a dissolving of the separation between "*It*/that tree" and "Buber on the tree trunk." For a brief moment, they merge into One, in a place that is love—God's place with you and me.

Buber is counseling you and me, sitting on this old tree. He is saying that there are two ways to look at existence: there is the *I* who looks at

3. Buber, *I and Thou*, 14.
4. Ibid.

creation and other humans as separate from me, and there is the *I* that looks at creation and other humans as *Thou*, in a connection without boundaries. Buber is teaching us that our life finds meaning in relationships. Recognizing this *I*-and-*Thou* connection with all creation brings us into deeper relationship with God.

The philosopher seems to have the mystical experience of merging with the tree, just as the Hindu yogi in deep contemplation has a brief experience of merging the self/*atman* with God/*Brahman*: the ultimate reality beyond all things.

In *Christianity and World Religions*, Christian theologian Heinrich von Stietencron describes graphically the rare experience of Raja Yoga and *Samadhi*, which is similar to Buber's experience meditating on the tree:

> After the withdrawal of the senses from the outer world, a parallel process begins with regard to the inner world. Here, too, the goal is gradually to shut off the multiplicity of ideas and to direct one's consciousness toward a single object of contemplation. If the effort succeeds, the state of absorption finally leads to a total view of the chosen object, encompassing every dimension of its reality.
>
> In the ultimate stage, the mind's penetration and experience of what it meditates on is so profound that the distance between subject and object is overcome, and at some point the separation breaks down. What happens then is usually described as a lighting-like comprehensive flash of awareness, which for the most part cannot be reproduced in speech. It is an experience in which all being telescopes into a single point. At the same time, the yogi has the overwhelming sense of radiant light.[5]

Perhaps the tree itself is beholding you and me sitting on this log. It is no wonder that many Native American people saw the tree as alive with a spirit presence and would come to the cottonwood for spiritual counsel.

5. Küng et al., *Christianity and World Religions*, 256.

Cottonwood Tree at Olancha, 2014. Author's collection.

Let me share a memory. It is 2009. I have had nine days in a hospital bed after extensive surgery. Monitors are beeping, medical people are poking and pulling, pain is coming and going. I close my eyes and remember the sound of the cottonwood tree. I see the shimmering, twisting, quaking leaves and I sense that God is very close. As I hold that foundational memory, I find sweet sleep.

The Freemont cottonwood will be found wherever you walk in the Owens Valley that is near water. I have contemplated its presence throughout the seasons: lush green in summer heat, shimmering gold in fall, naked with the look of death in winter, and that slight green patina of spring that announces that new life is coming.

Cottonwood trees have healed and fed the Owens Valley Paiute for centuries. The sweet sap can be eaten raw or cooked. The bitter bark can be cooked in strips or ground into powder. Many Native Americans like the sweet taste of the tree. Within the bark are the active biochemical elements of salicin and poulin, which have the effect of aspirin for fever or as an anti-inflammatory. A medicinal tea was made by the Paiutes from the bark and the leaves. The tea can also aid digestion, relieve coughs, and get rid of parasites and worms. It certainly is a wonder tree. The Hopi revere the cottonwood to such an extent that the Kachina images are carved from the aged wood. Kachinas are ancestor spirits and spirits of Nature that bring the seasonal rain to the Pueblo people.

All this, and the Freemont cottonwood sings too! In 2009, Bernie Krause of the California Academy of Science in San Francisco was in Utah listening for brown bats with a hydrophone. There was a strange interference. The closer the team came to an old cottonwood tree, the louder the interference. It had to be coming from the tree trunk. Krause drilled a hole into the base of the tree and inserted the listening device and recorded the sound. He brought the recording back to his studio and slowed it down and what he heard sounded distinctly like drums beating a syncopated rhythm. You can hear it for yourself in a video of Krause discussing the recording.[6] What was happening? The cells in the trunk were trying to maintain osmotic pressure. If there is not enough water, they suck in air. If the cells suck in too much air they burst. The sounds you heard are the cottonwood tree cells bursting. The dead cells are what create the tree rings. But there is more here. The cells die and the tree exudes sap, which draws insects, which draws birds. So you can see that within this old singing cottonwood tree a whole microhabitat is being created in the sound.

T. C. McLuhan includes this phenomenon in her compilation *Touch the Earth*:

> Did you know that trees talk? Well they do. They talk to each other, and they'll talk to you if you listen. Trouble is, white people don't listen. They never learned to listen to the Indians so I don't suppose they'll listen to other voices in nature. But I have learned a lot from trees: sometimes about the weather, sometimes about animals, sometimes about the Great Spirit.[7]

As you walk with me through the Owens Valley near Highway 395, welcome these new tree friends who will help you pay attention to the all-pervasive presence of the Holy One.

---

6. Krause, "Discovering a 'Singing' Tree," online at https://www.youtube.com/watch?v=uWkMWDSVZuQ.

7. McLuhan, *Touch the Earth*, 15.

6

Solitude and Silence in Cottonwood Canyon

The desert . . . empties you. Hence it is not a place wherein you can decide how you want to grow and change, but is a place that you undergo, expose yourself to, and have the courage to face. The idea is not so much that you do things there, but that things happen to you while there – silent, unseen, transforming things. The desert purifies you, almost against your will, through God's efforts. In the desert, what really occurs is a cosmic confrontation between God and the devil; though this happens within and through you. Your job is only to be have the courage to be there. The idea is that God does the work, providing you have the courage to show up.

—Fr. Ron Rolheiser, OMI[1]

Nothing resembles the language of God as much as silence.

—Meister Eckhart[2]

THE WIND IS BLOWING a horrific cloud of polluted dust thousands of feet into the sky above the ancient Owens Lake, east of the Sierra Nevada. I am driving north on Highway 395 past Olancha, at the southern tip of the lake, on the second day of my traditional Lenten desert retreat. I can see snow falling over the mountains of the Sierra Nevada as clouds darken slopes down to the valley floor.

---

1. Rolheiser, "Desert: A Place of Preparation."
2. Quoted from Roheiser, "Language of Silence."

I am heading north to Cottonwood Canyon, a place I have driven by dozens of times, but never visited. I cross the highway bridge over Cottonwood Creek and see the dry wash is riven with the scars of flash floods. On the right side of the road, beside Owens Lake, I see a band of aspen, willow and cottonwood trees marking the edge of an ancient shoreline. That is where the Paiute village of Sunga'va was located for six thousand years, recently excavated by archeologists of the University of California–Davis. Once, when the lake was high, this was a verdant place with abundant duck, deer, and antelope.

A mile south of that village lie the ruins of two charcoal kilns that were built by one Colonel Sherman. He also constructed a wooden flume that extended up the Sierra and denuded the slopes of the pinyon pine, which had been a key source of protein for the Native Americans of these parts. In the 1880s, Sherman had a profitable concern with his pinyon pine charcoal. It would be loaded at a landing not far from the site of the ancient village and small steamboats would carry it across the lake to the mining town of Swansea, where it was used to smelt silver ore. This morning the wind is brutal, rocking my 2002 Oldsmobile Bravada. I see a small sign for Cottonwood Road, turn left off Highway 395 and drive towards the power station at the foot of the mountains. The dirt road crosses the Los Angeles Aqueduct, which for a hundred years has been draining the Sierra snowmelt into booming Los Angeles.

The road continues left toward Cottonwood Canyon and alternates between graded gravel and paved asphalt for the next five miles. I guess the erosion of the road is further evidence of the violent storms that wash through this canyon. The road climbs, twists and turns, and a wondrous sight unfolds before me, making it difficult to focus on driving. Huge granite walls loom higher and higher in beautiful and strange formations of red and orange. I am entering into the heart of the Sierra. Tree-topped crests covered in snow rise before me. Once I have entered the shelter of the canyon, the rushing desert windstorm has been blocked out. Silence.

There are numerous clusters of green oak trees now and there is the sound of rushing water from the snowmelt thousands of feet above me. The sun is warm, the air still and not a single human can be seen. Suddenly a bobcat rushes past me. I am a stranger in this place where even the birds are silent. Deeper and deeper I drive into the twisting canyon. There is an old clapboard green building, maybe a Forest Service residence. But no one is home. This place is crowded with campers and fishermen during the fishing season; it's a place to retreat from the intense summer heat in the valley below. I park at the end of the road where the Cottonwood Trail begins. The trail follows an ancient Native American trade route over the Sierra Nevada and is now popular with summer hikers.

I am at rest. My busy mind finds solace here in the solitude of this canyon. A spirit of gratitude to God flows through my heart.

I remember that there are also ghosts here: echoes of the Paiute families who flourished in the canyon for thousands of years. There is also the hateful dream-echo of gunfire, for here at the canyon's mouth a Paiute chief and his warriors desperately defended themselves from the white settlers. On March 19, 1863, Lieutenant Doughty and twenty soldiers from Camp Independence (near the present county seat of Inyo County, forty miles south of Bishop), with twenty civilians, tracked thirty-seven Paiutes moving south of Manzanar. W. A. Chalfant in his *The Story of Inyo* takes up the tale.

> The trail was followed . . . to a point two miles or so north of Cottonwood Creek, when a bullet through a man's hat gave warning of the nearness of the foe. The Indians were found strongly posted in a ravine about five miles south of the head of Owens Lake. They were dislodged, and a running fight ensued, the whole action taking about four hours before they made a last stand on the lakeshore, not far from the mouth of Cottonwood Creek. . . . Lieutenant Doughty was dismounted by accidentally shooting his own horse through the head. Corporal McKenna received a load of buckshot in his foot from another accidental shot and an Indian arrow in his chest. When he fell, a Paiute known as Chief Butcherknife ran up to finish him, but was slain. More casualties to the whites resulted from bad handling of their own weapons than from those of the foe.
>
> With sixteen dead on the field, the remaining Indians sought refuge in the waters of the lake. A strong wind blowing from the east interfered with their escape by swimming, and one after another was killed in the light of a full moon rising over the eastern mountains.[3]

3. Chalfant, *Story of Inyo*, 187.

39

Cottonwood Creek, Cottonwood Canyon, 2009. Author's collection.

During the night, a single Paiute escaped westward into Cottonwood Canyon. Archaeological artifacts from this battle were discovered on the northwestern shore of Owens Lake in June 2013.

I am remembering that battle and other struggles of the native people as I walk past a grove of oak trees. Somewhere near these trees is where native ceremonies such as weddings and naming rituals still take place.

I am walking around boulders and old willow and cottonwood trees, nearing the rushing waters of Cottonwood Creek. I find a flat rock on which to sit in the warm sunshine. The air is calm. Tree leaves rustle and flutter. Water flows and tumbles over boulders in a hypnotic rhythm that captivates me. My consciousness dissolves into this scene, mind empties, and breath slows. God is very close, embracing me with love and peace. I gaze into the water and remember these words from the *Tao Te Ching*:

> The supreme good is like water,
>
> which nourishes all things without trying to.
>
> It is content with the low places that people disdain.
>
> Thus it is like the Tao.[4]

I imagine someone else sitting on that flat rock over there beneath the towering sycamore tree. His long hair and beard flow over a rumpled, sackcloth robe. He is also focused on the water flowing from the mountain above into the low, receptive basins. He is Lao Tzu.

Said to be a mythical figure, historians tell us that Lao Tzu lived in the sixth century BCE. The great Zhou Dynasty of China had disintegrated during the Warring States period. Do you remember the great suffering, deaths and political chaos following the breakup of Yugoslavia at the end of the last century? On a far greater scale this is what happened in China many centuries before: wholesale slaughter, burning cities, power in the hands of ruthless warlords. How could the pieces of China be put back together? Two answers came forth. First, the philosopher Confucius advocated a return to the core values of early Zhou feudalism. The other answer came from Lao Tzu and Taoism: a withdrawal to nature and simplicity.

I imagine Lao Tzu sitting on the rock next to me beside Cottonwood Creek. We gaze together at the water flowing from the mountain high above. Water is fluid and can penetrate the finest cavities. It flows to the low, receptive places, breaking down the hardest rock. The Tao is like water, nourishing all creatures without controlling them.

Lao Tzu looked to the patterns and flow in nature, giving him intuitive insight about the nature of Ultimate Reality (the Tao) and how we should best live.

4. Mitchell, trans., *Tao Te Ching*, ch. 8.

There was something formless and perfect

before the universe was born.

It is serene. Empty.

Solitary. Unchanging.

Infinite. Eternally present.

It is the mother of the universe.

For lack of a better name,

I call it the Tao.[5]

When I reflect on the Tao with my students of World Religions I usually get blank faces. We arrive at this point after having studied the vivid personalities of the Hindu deities and Buddhist bodhisattvas. The Western mind struggles with the mystery of the Tao. As if to counter our Western need for categories and descriptions of the Holy, Lao Tzu short-circuits our linear thinking. As we read the *Tao Te Ching*, he offers us paradoxes to guide us into mystery. He teaches us that silence and solitude in nature is the best experience for communion with the Holy, the Tao.

> Standing in front of it, you will not discover its beginning; standing behind it, you will not discover its end. Only standing within its ongoing creative action will you feel the enfolding embrace of the Tao.[6]

This brings to mind a thread from Western theology: although Moses did receive the name of God on Mount Sinai, the Jewish people traditionally have avoided use of the holy name. Indeed, the names Jehovah and Yahweh were derived from unpronounceable groups of Hebrew letters, so when the lector arrived at them in the holy texts he would simply bow his head in silence. The mystic Martin Buber taught that when we speak of God, we mean "the essential mystery, the unknowable, and the paradox of paradoxes."[7]

Then the leading theologian of late medieval times, Thomas Aquinas, wrote a lot about the nature of God, giving us the classic five proofs of the existence of God. But as he grew older, he gave in to the Mystery, saying, "we cannot contemplate how God is, but only how God is not. This is the ultimate in human knowledge of God: to know that we do not know him."

5. Ibid., ch. 25.

6. McCauley, "Deep Mystery of God."

7. Ibid.

At the end of his life, he is said to have confessed, "All that I have hitherto written seems to me nothing but straw."[8]

I have had the same experience. As I grow in friendship with God, there are many times when I have confessed that though I have been a priest for forty-two years I feel I know nothing, understand nothing. That is overstating the case. I *do* know my foundation experiences of the love and goodness of God.

> The Master leads
> by emptying people's minds
> and filling their cores,
> by weakening their ambition
> and toughening their resolve.
> He helps people lose everything
> they know, everything they desire,
> and creates confusion
> in those who think that they know.[9]

Cottonwood Canyon looking toward dust storm, 2009. Author's collection.

8. Ibid.
9. Mitchell, trans., *Tao Te Ching*, ch. 3.

You will recognize some similarities between the teachings of Lao Tzu and Zen Buddhism. When Buddhism arrived in China it blended with Taoism to form Zen.

Those howling, jostling winds are still blowing out on Highway 395. But in this protective womb of canyon cliffs the air is still and the quiet serene. Lao Tzu guides us to quieting our minds, practicing "no mind," as the constant storm of voices and sounds assault us on the outside. In silent meditation, on this rock, I go to that deep place where God's love flows. I cannot put words to these experiences, even though I try to write about them later in my journal. What I do want to remember is the intuitive encounter with Holy Mystery.

Ron Rolheiser encourages us to make these retreats into silence and solitude:

> There is a huge silence undergirding us and inside of us that is trying to draw us into itself. To enter that silence is to enter the reality of God and the reality of our real communion with each other. For this reason, all great religious traditions and all great spiritual writers emphasize the need for silence at times in our lives . . . As Thomas Merton put it, there is a hidden wholeness at the heart of things, and that hidden wholeness can only be discovered if we get to the deepest level of things. And the language we need to get there is the language of silence - the language of God and the language of intimacy.[10]

If you practice the Christian method of centering prayer, meditation with Lao Tzu will sound familiar. As you sit in solitude and quiet in the morning, before the start of a busy day, you can follow the instruction of Father Thomas Keating:

> We close our eyes to what is going on around us and within us. When you become aware of thoughts, return ever-so-gently to the sacred word. "Thoughts" is an umbrella term for every perception, including sense perceptions, feelings, images, memories, reflections and commentaries . . . He leads us by means of sacred experiences to the experience of emptiness. Anything that we perceive of God can only be a radiance of His presence and not God as He is Himself.[11]

---

10. Rolheiser, "Language of Silence."

11. Keating, *Open Mind, Open Heart*, 139–41.

I drive out of Cottonwood Canyon, trimmed with the spiritual ballast of God's Grace. I drive back into the wild winds of the desert.

7

Finding Solitude in a Miner's Cabin

By touching the center of our solitude, we sense that we have been touched by loving hands.

—Henri Nouwen[1]

The hot June desert wind buffets my car as I drive the sandy road east toward the Inyo Mountains. I park at the end of the road and aim at the ruins of a miner's stone cabin that I have spotted. I slowly climb the hillside past spindly branches of creosote, which brush against my Levis. The sun sets early behind the Sierra Nevada and it is hard to see ahead in the looming shadows. Almost there. My heart stops at the doorway. Loud rattles and hissing. Rattlesnake! This cabin is already occupied. I leap away and roll back down the hillside. Boy, that was a close one! Thank God for rattles! Of course, hindsight speaks with authority: sunset is when the snakes begin to emerge after a hot day in the desert. I should have known better.

Summer is not the best time for contemplative desert walks. I normally time my visits between November and March. The following fall I revisit the miner's cabin. It is a brilliant sunny day, but a much more sensible 50 °F. It is very important that I be here.

---

1. Nouwen, *Essential Henri Nouwen*, 8.

Miner's stone cabin with fireplace, Reward Mine, 2010. Author's collection.

Driving nine miles north of the town of Lone Pine, which nestles at the foot of Mt. Whitney, I look for the ruins of the Manzanar Japanese American Relocation Camp on the west side of the highway. On the right a small street sign indicates Manzanar Reward Road. I turn onto the paved way, which runs through the remains of a World War II airfield. Continuing east towards the Inyo Mountains, I cross the Owens River Aqueduct, which carries away most of the Sierra snowmelt to the thirsty homes of Los Angeles. The road continues past the cottonwood and willow trees lining the bed of the Owens River, which has recently been revitalized with water courtesy of a lawsuit against Los Angeles Department of Water and Power. The pavement ends and I am driving through open range. I must watch out for cows here. In autumn the sagebrush landscape will be thick with the black shapes of Angus cows and tiny clumps of newborn calves. The road continues east. I look for the north-south elevation, which is all that remains of the narrow-gauge Carson and Colorado Railroad that ran three hundred miles to Carson City, Nevada. I pause at the intersection of the road with the ghost railroad bed and imagine the settlement that flourished here in the early 1900s. Before the water was siphoned off, Manzanar was a verdant orchard of apples, pears, and peaches. The railroad station at this intersection was where the crops would be loaded and shipped. I know that there were also a general store, saloon, and one-room schoolhouse here. But all of this has disappeared in the desert sands.

I continue east to a 'Y' in the road. A sign tells me I have arrived at Owenyo Road. I bear left toward the mountains. The gnarled folds of the barren mountains are scars from volcanic lava flows and violent upthrusts of the earth's crust. Here is the historic settlement of Reward, which has been mined for silver and gold almost continually since the 1860s. The road narrows and I see a canyon ravine on the right. I find a level, open space to park as the road becomes very rocky here. To the right I can see the ruins of a multilevel mill where the ore was processed. If you look carefully up into the mountainside you will see the remains of the tram that brought the ore down to this mill, and a rock-lined miner's trail. To the left you will see the ruins of several rock cabins. I walk the road that goes left and around the mountain toward another ravine. Look carefully to your right and you will see the remains of a rock structure built into the mountainside. It is autumn and the snakes should be sleeping. As you walk around the ruin you will see a marvelously constructed fireplace still standing. If you enter the old cabin you can appreciate the careful stonework, and there is a magnificent view of the Sierra through what remains of a window. I love this place.

I used to fear being alone. But something changed in my life and I became more aware of the presence of the Holy One. The desert gave me that gift. So I relish places like this cabin and the solitude I experience here.

On this November morning, cold wind stings my ears and nose. I sit on a rocky ledge inside the cabin and examine the way it was built. No mortar. Carefully positioned rocks comprise walls that have lasted 140 years. The fireplace warmed the solitary miner who sheltered here from wind, snow, and rain, as he collapsed exhausted on his little cot after working twelve hours or more in the mine.

How I hunger for this place! I must always take a day to decompress before I come here. How busy are our lives and busy our minds! Cell phones, emails, messages, to-do lists. It is endless. I am forever anxious about what I haven't done yet, about whom I have let down, about expectations I have created and not met.

As Ron Rolheiser expresses in his book *The Holy Longing*, we are forever restless and yearning for something. Within that whirlpool of busyness and fatigue and projects that churn our life with restlessness, we yearn for some place of solitude and quiet where we can rest. That yearning comes from somewhere inside us: soul. Our stomach grumbles to tell us we are hungry. Our soul aches for solitude.

We will find a place somewhere, a cabin or condominium at the ocean or in Palm Springs. We will block out time in the planner. We will pack some food and good books, determined to leave the iPhone and iPad at home—but then we remember some of our books are loaded on those machines.

It is hard to program silence and solitude. From my experience through the many health crises of our son Erik, solitude finds us, grabs us, and pulls us in. I think it was back in 1990 that I was first led out here into the Owens Valley. The desert trips began as hikes. I tried to do too much physically. But after a while (it took at least a day), walking alone, pausing and taking in the landscape and its features such as this miner's cabin, something would perk up inside me. Something awakened to the Presence. After I had done the hikes that I had planned and had taken some real rest, I could walk more slowly. And then simply stop and sit. And *be*. I would eventually arrive at a point where anxiety about projects undone, voices of wants on which I had to deliver, quieted into the background

Rolheiser writes:

> Solitude is not something we turn on like a water faucet. It needs a body and mind slowed down enough to be attentive to the present moment. We are in solitude when, as Merton says, we fully taste the water we are drinking, feel the warmth of the blankets, and are restful enough to be content inside our own skin. We don't often accomplish this, despite sincere effort, but we need to keep making new beginnings.[2]

I believe that deep within you and me there is a place where God has touched us and held us very close. Rolheiser continues:

> Long before memory, long before we ever remember touching or loving or kissing anyone or anything, or being touched by anything or anybody in this world, there is a different kind of memory, the memory of being gently touched by loving hands. When our ear is pressed to God's heart—to the breast of all that is good, true and beautiful—we hear a certain heartbeat and we remember,

---

2. Rolheiser, "Longing for Solitude."

remember in some inchoate place, at a level beyond thought, that
we were once kissed by God.[3]

Is this what happens to me when the desert quiets my mind and that busy
mental computer winds down to a faint hum? Am I remembering this primal embrace of the Holy before I was born? I forgot, but when all is quiet
and still, in solitude, my heart warms in this desert space and I remember.

Solitude helps us to remember the kiss and embrace and touch of the
Holy. In the busyness of routine and commitments and responsibilities, I
forget. You forget. When I sit on the rock in this cabin ruin, dry desert wind
flows through my being, the vast landscape opens up spilling out toward
the Sierra, and I am possessed by this memory. Spanish mystic Saint John
of the Cross once defined solitude as "Bringing the mild into harmony with
the mild"[4] I think that means that we will remember the primal embrace of
the Holy One when we enter into solitude and silence. I find that this is the
place where I can offer up those inner voices echoing anger, jealousy, frus-
tration, and disappointment. When the desert turns our face to the present
moment, we become mild, as Saint John invites, and we sense the enfolding
embrace of the Holy One that had never let us go.

To reach that inner space of peace, joy, love, and hope, I come out here
to the desert. She is the primal womb of most spiritual wisdom. The remembering comes as a surprise. I cannot conjure or manipulate it. But I do have
to do the work of retreating and journeying to a place set apart. Then, in time,
the wind of the Spirit will catch me and lift me up. The pilot light of memory
is lit and I can carry that light with me back into the world of projects, duty,
and responsibilities, and become that embrace of God for all creation.

3. Ibid.

4. Quoted from Rolheiser, "Domestic Monastery."

8

Revelations in a Cave

وَإِذِ ٱعۡتَزَلۡتُمُوهُمۡ وَمَا يَعۡبُدُونَ إِلَّا ٱللَّهَ فَأۡوُوٓاْ إِلَى ٱلۡكَهۡفِ يَنشُرۡ لَكُمۡ
رَبُّكُم مِّن رَّحۡمَتِهِۦ وَيُهَيِّئۡ لَكُم مِّنۡ أَمۡرِكُم مِّرۡفَقًا ﴿١٦﴾

When ye turn away from them and the things they worship other than Allah,
betake yourselves to the Cave: Your Lord will shower His mercies on you and
disposes of your affair towards comfort and ease.

—QURAN, 18:16 ("THE CAVE")[1]

THERE IS A DISUSED mine, a cave really, that for me has taken on mythical
qualities over the years, because, though I have searched among the ruins of
the mining camp of Reward at the foot of the Inyo Mountains, it has eluded
me. It is supposed to be there but I find only dead ends.

At the end of the Manzanar-Reward Road going east from Highway
395, the foundations for the mill that processed the silver-gold ore occupy
the south side of the road. The previous chapter guided you among the
ruins of the rock-walled miners' cabins on the west side of the camp. I feel I
know my way around here, but where is the fabled mine tunnel big enough
for a truck to drive into? Not a clue.

One day, as I sit on a rock drinking Gatorade near the ruins of the old
mill, a beat-up silver Toyota truck barrels towards me in a swirling cloud
of dust. Two young men wave to me as they turn onto the rocky road that
climbs past the miners' cabins and curves around to the north side of the

1. Yusuf Ali, trans., *Meaning of the Holy Qur'an*, 711.

mountain. Here is a clue. Where are those guys going? I began to hike up that dirt road. You need good hiking boots here with high tops to support your ankles. The road takes me up to the ravine on the north side, and where it straightens out I can see a huge mine dump ahead. All that rock and dirt tell me a sizeable mine has to be up here somewhere. It is a slow, slogging walk. No matter how much I work out on the treadmill at LA Fitness to get ready for this terrain, I am at four thousand feet and the altitude always makes my legs rubbery for a couple of days.

Mining town of Reward, ca.1890. County of Inyo, Eastern California Museum.

I see clusters of "rat hole" mine shafts poking out of the side of the mountain. Going back to the 1860s, the prospectors who worked this mountain dug a complex honeycomb of tunnels. I am well aware of the wisdom of the desert guides who always warn us against entering mines. But maybe this is different. As I approach the enormous mound of tailings and excavated dirt, another cloud of dust announces the return of the battered pickup. The youthful explorers are bouncing back down the hill to me.

"Is that the famous tunnel I have heard about?" I ask. "Can you really drive your truck into it? Is it safe?"

The driver, with a mouthful of chewing tobacco, responds,

"Sure. We just went in about two thousand feet. There is a place at the end where you can turn around. The tunnel is fine. But wait a bit for our dust to settle."

Confirmation at last! I am excited.

As I approach the entrance, I remember that this area was last mined in 1981. By then they were using skip-loaders rather than picks and shovels. I can see some of the drill holes where dynamite would be placed in a semicircular pattern to blast into the mountain. Bright yellow and red spray paint marks a recent visit of a geologist recording the present path of the vein. I walk into the wide shaft. It is solid rock, no supports. Looks stable.

Some warnings: always enter a tunnel or cave keeping to one side, in case some critter living in there wants to make a fast escape. Also, throw in some rocks to test for snakes lurking in the shadows. Wear a hardhat. Take with you two flashlights and extra batteries. You can get a headlamp at the True Value Hardware Store in Lone Pine.

As I enter for the first time, I am nervous and cautious, and I am alone. It is always best to be exploring with someone else. As I walk, sunlight shimmers over the vein of ore embedded in the rock. The ground slopes downhill. A turn in the tunnel leads into darkness. Time for the flashlight. As I walk deeper, the sound of blood rushing in my ears beats like a drum. The slightest sound is magnified here. I try something. I turn off the flashlight. Total darkness. I cannot see my hand in front of my face. Silence. Darkness. I turn the light back on and walk a little further. On my right, a recess marks where some ore was dug out and an old wooden ladder hangs there, leading to an upper level of drifts in this riddled mountain. Never climb such ladders; they are invariably rotten deathtraps. But they do give us clues about the grueling work done here all those years ago. I walk the two thousand feet to the end of the tunnel where I find the turnaround. Cold wind grabs me; it is certainly coming from somewhere: perhaps another tunnel from the other side of the mountain. I turn to walk back, but hesitate because I still want to fully know this darkness and silence. I cannot tell you that at this point I am experiencing the close presence of God because I am anxious and apprehensive, but I sure want God close to me now!

Miles of tunnels fan out from this point. The darkness fascinates me. A rock falls; sound reverberates. If I were in another state of mind, my neck hairs would bristle and goose bumps would cover my body. What is down there in the lower levels of darkness? Ghost hunters could use sensors to test for spirits of miners who died violently. Tommyknockers, the legendary gremlins of the mines, could be up to mischief. These thoughts occur to me now as I am writing, but I am grateful I did not think them during my visit!

As I walk uphill toward the sunlight, I feel more secure. I slowly rub my hands over the rock walls and enjoy the variety of colors. Scintillating quartz crystals thrust outward. I am thinking about the ancient desert mystics who would seek out caves like this. Some were looking for refuge from trouble; others sought solitude to meditate on God's presence.

Miners at the Reward Mine, ca. 1880. County of Inyo, Eastern California Museum.

The prophet Abraham had two sons. His first son, Ishmael, born of Hagar, was displaced by the younger son, Isaac, born of wife Sarah.

> As for Ishmael, I have heeded you. I hereby bless him. I will make him fertile and exceedingly numerous. He shall be the father of twelve chieftains, and I will make of him a great nation. But my covenant I will maintain with Isaac. (Genesis 17:20–21)

Abraham took Ishmael and Hagar to the desert valley of Becca (Mecca) to spare them Sarah's jealousy. The Holy Quran says that Abraham and Ishmael built the Kabah there as a shrine, at the place where Adam first worshipped God. It is written that God told Abraham that the Kabah should be a place of pilgrimage. And this is whence, perhaps two thousand years later, the prophet Mohammed took to the cool recesses of a cave outside Mecca. Mohammed would frequent this retreat for the silence and solitude it afforded, meditating and praying to Allah (which means "The God," the same God worshipped by Christians and Jews).

Mohammed had to withdraw from the noise and crowds of the city. Mecca had become a wealthy trading capital and a place of pilgrimage for devotees of animist religions. The Kabah (in fact, the remains of an ancient meteor) was the locus of their devotions. Images of 360 different fertility gods surrounded this ancient spiritual space—a new god for each day. Money-eyed pilgrims would arrive in a constant stream while the flourishing city remained indifferent to its poor, who were left to scrounge a living from the garbage dumps of the rich. This depressed Mohammed and made his retreats to the cave all the more necessary. One day, praying in the cool shade of the cave, Mohammed had a visitor. Within the darkness, the angel Gabriel spoke:

> Proclaim in the name of the Lord and Cherisher,
>
> Who created man, out of a mere clot of congealed blood:
>
> Proclaim! And thy Lord is most bountiful-
>
> He who taught the use of the pen taught man that which he knew not. (Quran 96:1–5 ["The Clot"])[2]

Mohammed was the last of a chain of prophets who came to restore the true religion. Thus Islam is not an upstart following; it is the restoration of the original monotheism revealed to Adam, Noah, Abraham and all the earlier prophets. At the age of twenty-five, Mohammed had married Khadijah, a rich widow, fifteen years his senior. It was when he was forty, in the month of Ramadan, AD 610, that he first received the call from God through the angel Gabriel in the cave of Hira. He returned home deeply shaken. But Khadijah encouraged him to continue to listen to the voice of God. For the next twenty-three years these revelations continued with the same theme: the one true God was calling his people to Islam—a word that means "trusting surrender to God." Mohammed described what it was like when Allah spoke to him:

> Revelation sometimes came like the sound of a bell; that is the most painful way. When it ceases I have remembered what was said. Sometimes it is an angel who talks to me like a human and I remember what he says.[3]

Tradition holds that Mohammed could not read or write, so his followers had to grab whatever they could write on whenever he had these

---

2. Ibid., 1672–73.

3. Schimmel, *And Muhammad Is His Messenger*, 11.

unexpected visits from the angel communicating the Divine Word. What the angel was communicating was the original Word of God from the *Kitab*, the Eternal Word in Heaven. Jews and Christians had received this same word, but they had perverted it by their factionalism. Christians deviated from this Word in that they taught that God's Son had died on the cross for the sins of the world.

Now Allah was imparting the True Word, guidance for the Straight Path.

Once Mohammed had shared these revelations with his wife and family, he began to preach publicly. But his words threatened the economy of the great city of Mecca since he condemned the idolatry of the 360 fertility gods who drew all those pilgrims. However, some visitors from the city of Medina, 250 miles to the north, liked what they heard and invited him to come to their city to solve their political and social problems.

This meant that Mohammed and his followers had to leave Mecca secretly. But in a scene reminding us of when Pharaoh chased after Moses and his people in the exodus, Mohammed and his old friend Abu Bakr hid in the cave of Hira, where God worked a miracle to protect them: an acacia tree sprang up in front of the cave, a dove flew over and wove its nest and laid its eggs, and a spider spread its web over the cave's entrance to hide Mohammed from his enemies.

The journey to Medina is known as the Hijrah Migration. It took place in 622 CE, which now marks the beginning of the Muslim calendar.

In my World Religions class, I contrast the devotion that Jews and Christians have for their scriptures with the devotion Muslims have for the Quran. Jews and Christians have their books through many translations: Hebrew to Greek to Latin to most of the world's modern languages. But there are only fragmentary portions extant of the original Hebrew and Christian books. Muslims believe that the Quran they hold in their hands, written in the classic Kufic Arabic script, is the very Word of God as given to Mohammed. They have direct access to God in their meditation and study of the Quran. A translation is not a Quran.

For Muslims, the Holy Quran is a sacred object to be treated with great reverence. For instance, it should not be held below the belt and is never placed in a pile under other books. Traditionally, Muslims read the Quran by sitting on the floor, with the Quran suspended on a *kursi* or chair. Before reading or meditating with the Quran, you must be ritually purified. Very traditional Muslims teach that non-Muslims should not touch the Quran.

I have a copy of the Quran given to me about twenty years ago by the Muslim Students Association of Saddleback College. It reminds me of the Oxford Annotated Study Bible. Each page has the traditional words in Arabic on the left side with an English translation to the right. An authorized commentary by a respected imam runs below the sacred text.

If you are Christian or Jewish, as you read the Quran you find old spiritual friends there: Adam, Noah, and Abraham. Each book is a *surah*. There is even a surah of Mary, which describes a birth narrative of Jesus very different from that found in the Gospels. Jesus has a significant presence in the Quran. He is a messiah, an anointed messenger of God. He is portrayed as a remote ascetic, and he is deeply revered. Muslims believe that on the Day of Judgment Jesus and Mary will appear by the Seat of Allah.

Muslim Sufi, Christian, and Jewish mystics find common ground in meditating on the presence of God as an invitation to loving friendship with the Holy One. If I read passages from any of these mystic poets, without knowing their particular religious tradition, I am struck by the fact they have all encountered the same loving, compassionate Presence. As an example, listen to the words of the Muslim Sufi mystic Hafiz:

> All the talents of God are within you.
> How could this be otherwise
> When your soul
> Derived from His genes!
> I love that expression,
> "All the talents of God are within you."
> Sometimes Hafiz cannot help but to applaud
> Certain words that rise from my depths
> Like the scent of a lover's body.
> Hold this book close to your heart
> For it contains wonderful secrets.[4]

4. Hafiz, *Gift*, 207.

9

Finding Your True Self in the Desert

The desert has a deep personality. It has a voice; and God speaks through its personality and voice. Great elders in all ages . . . have sought the desert and heard its voice.

—L. L. Nunn, founder of Deep Springs College[1]

It is October 2005. I gently close the door to Room 20 and step into the cold morning darkness. This room was where John Wayne slept when he made his last film. The parking lot of the Dow Villa Motel in Lone Pine, California, is filled with cars sporting an array of out-of-state license plates. I start my Olds Bravada and slowly move out onto Highway 395 and turn left at the signal onto Whitney Portal Road. I maneuver up the winding mountain road that eventually leads to the base camp for climbing Mount Whitney. Passing through a gap in the Alabama Hills, I continue toward the Sierra Nevada, turning right on Movie Road. I must drive with extra caution here because two deer just ran across the highway. I drive north on this wide dirt road, park the car, and step out to crunching sand and a slight, cold breeze. I face the Sierra as a new day of life begins. Dawn light emerges from the east out of Death Valley, illuminating the Sierra with soft purples and pinks. A cottontail rabbit dashes into a clump of sagebrush.

Silence. My soul awakens in this special place that joins heaven and earth, this spiritually "thin" place, between darkness and light, between the past and the future. This present moment. This present breath.

1. Quoted from the college's homepage, http://www.deepsprings.edu/home.

The dawning of a new day is when the first songs of praise and adoration ring from the rich storehouse of spiritualties of the world. Similarly each morning many traditional Shoshone will face the rising sun and sing a *prayer to Appah.* They believe that the rays of the sun carry their words up to *Appah*, Our Father, Our Creator.

The Hindu has morning prayers too. This short prayer is an invitation to dissolve in devotion to God.

> I meditate in the morning, upon the greatly exalted form of Sun God,
>
> Whose plane is Rig Veda, whose body is Yajur Veda,
>
> Whose rays are Sama Veda, who is the source of light,
>
> And whose unimaginable form does the work of holy trinity.[2]

The Muslim also prays this prayer for a new day, the *Salatu-l-Fajr*:

> Glory be to You, O God, and Yours is the praise and blessed is Your name, and exalted is Your majesty, and there is no god besides You. I seek the refuge of God from the condemned devil. In the name of God, Most Gracious, Most Merciful.[3]

In my own Christian voice I pray from Psalm 118:24:

> This is the day the Lord has made, let us rejoice and be glad in it!

The sun warms my back, desert wind encircles me, and The Holy surrounds me in love and peace. The desert calls me deeper into God's unconditional embrace.

January 1978. The panic attacks always seemed to strike me before Saturday midnight, the worst of times because I was supposed to be bright, alert, and ready on Sunday morning to preach and to celebrate the Eucharist at St. Mary's Parish in Laguna Beach, California.

That Saturday afternoon I had worked out hard at the Laguna Beach Health Club, curling fifty-five-pound dumbbells, heavy weights pressing the limit of my endurance. After dinner I had jogged two miles into the hills around our home, hoping that the endorphins would take over, that the natural narcotic would bring me sweet sleep. But not this night. After

---

2. "Pratha Smarana Surya Stotram" ("Morning Prayer to Sun God"), quoted from http://www.hindupedia.com/en/Pratha_Smarana_Surya_Stotram.

3. Quoted from http://www.islamanswering.com/subpage.php?s=article&aid=1423.

tossing and turning in bed for two hours, I try that relaxation exercise—do you remember it? I am filled with sand, there are holes in my feet, and the sand is slowly emptying out of my body. However, the panic attack has a firm hold on my body. It possesses me. The pain in my legs, the titillating prickly sweat of anxiety covers me. I feel my pulse: 110 beats a minute. My mind churns as if I had had four cups of coffee. I try to remember quiet places in my memory, but my body resists. Three hours of this and finally I get up, walk into the living room, and jog in place until I can no longer stand up and I am covered in sweat. By three the panic attack has left my body and I sleep for four tiny hours. On Sunday morning my mind is moving through thick fog. I cannot go on living this way.

These panic attacks had to mean something. Was I heading for a nervous breakdown? A friend suggested I get some counseling to find out what my body was telling me.

The following week I climbed the stairs to the office of psychiatrist Dr. Robert Phillips, MD, in Orange, California. I already knew Dr. Bob from when he had attended services at St. Mary's. I remembered his quiet, Buddha-like presence as he sat in a wheelchair in a corner of the church. He always had some pithy, humorous reflection on my sermon to share with me.

I entered his office wondering what I was getting into. What inner doors would I be opening? Should I be afraid? I had been a priest for seven years at this point and had counseled many people through marriage difficulties and crises. I would invite them to live in the light and to be open to God and what was going on in their lives, to live in a place "Where no secrets are hid," and to share their struggles. But now this was a different situation: I was the one seeking help. I sat on the couch in Dr. Bob's office at that first clinical encounter and observed him as he wheeled himself closer to me.

In those days, he liked to smoke thin cigarettes wrapped in very dark paper. He told me that he had originally prepared to become a pediatrician at Columbia University Medical School. One day he attended a lecture on multiple sclerosis and he recognized that he himself had the early stages of the disease. He changed to psychiatry as a form of medicine that he could practice from a wheelchair. Dr. Bob was a heavily built man, with long, straight grey hair tumbling over his shirt collar. Bushy eyebrows were like exclamation points to his penetrating questions. He presented himself to me as an Orthodox Jewish–Episcopalian Christian–Zen

Buddhist–Gestalt therapist. Moses, Jesus, and Siddhartha wove in and out of our conversations.

Health insurance was more generous in the 1970s. I could see Dr. Bob several times a week. Eventually I was lying down on the office couch, in traditional Freudian repose, staring at the ceiling as he guided me deeper into reflective consciousness. I must have been boring to him most of the time. He did not have much to say to me until the end of those forty-five minute sessions. Sometimes I would find him nodding off. Another time I looked up and saw that he was flipping through pages of the New Yorker at his desk, while I poured out my soul to him! I was angry and chastised him for his indifference.

He responded, "When you have said something interesting, you will hear from me." I almost walked out the door, never to return. But I wanted to know what was going on with these panic attacks. Why this restless energy?

As I look back at those sessions of psychoanalysis, it is hard to re-member Dr. Bob's revelations. I recall trying to write down an insightful observation at the end of a session. Nevertheless, as I tried to write, I could not recall the words that he had said only five minutes previously. It was as if some mysterious force did not want me to remember what had been revealed. Just two insights have remained with me all these years. They con-cern the power of the addictive voice, and the struggle to break free from the False Self in order to embrace the True Self.

Self-knowledge opened from inner recesses. I had long been a com-pulsive liar. I had stolen books from the USC Doheny Library, had been arrested for grand theft, and had been expelled from school. Webs of lies and deception trapped me.

I can remember Dr. Bob saying something like, "Brad, you are an in-telligent person and part of your problem is you have this very clever voice that talks you into lies and deception. If you weren't a priest, you would have been successful at white collar crime until you were caught."

"Is there any hope for me?" I pleaded.

"No. You are hopeless. That inner voice is just too powerful. It will probably pull you down into some destructive addiction."

"No hope? Is there no way out of this?"

"Your only hope is to see that you are powerless in trying to manage your life. Much of your anxiety comes from trying to control the events and people around you. When you finally let go, help will come."

"You sound like a priest telling me I need to let go to find God."

"Right now I am the only priest you have to guide you through this wilderness. I hear you preaching on Sunday about faith and God's grace, but in all of our time together, you sound like someone trying to run your own universe. And you are experiencing the emotional expense of living in that mirage."

The contemporary theologian and psychologist, and author of many books about the addictive condition, Gerald May, writes:

> Addiction exists wherever persons are internally compelled to give energy to things that are not their true desires . . . Addiction is a state of compulsion, obsession, or preoccupation that enslaves a person's will and desire. Addiction sidetracks and eclipses the energy of our deepest, truest desire for love and goodness. We succumb because the energy of our desire becomes attached, nailed, to specific behaviors, objects or people.[4]

Dr. Bob was underlining the teaching of all world religions: the Holy One birthed us for love and freedom. Addiction blocks this loving, free relationship with the Creator. My psychiatrist wanted me to recognize that I was helpless to fix my situation on my own, and my need for Divine Amazing Grace. Only years later, it would be in my desert encounters with the Holy that I would understand what he was trying to tell me.

Over many months of psychotherapy, the possessive power of the False Self was also made clear to me. Memories of childhood revealed experiences of deep, genuine nurturing from my mother; of being touched, held, spoken to softly, reassured in scary times. Every night before sleep, Mom would read to me. She was generous and playful. I was surrounded in a circle of love from my parents.

I think it began around seventh grade at Wilson Junior High School in Pasadena: those hormones and the initial pushback and resistance to my parents. They began to trade love and their approval for my good performance in school: good grades in Latin, math, and science, playing the cello in orchestra, rising above the crowd in student government, and lettering in football. The more successful I became in school, the more I received

4. May, *Addiction and Grace*, 14.

parental approval. I learned who the popular kids were and worked my way into their friendship. By ninth grade I saw that my value depended on what I could do, what I had, who I knew, and what others thought of me. I was well on the way to constructing the False Self.

I asked my long-time friend Dr. Lawrence Budner, MD, a child psychiatrist, to share with me his thoughts about the construction of the False Self. Here is what he said:

> During the first months of an infant's life, the mother's devoted care and responsiveness gives the infant the sense that the world is safe, reliable, and loving. Misunderstandings between them are quickly corrected. However, at some point, the infant expresses a wish or an impulse and gets a response that hurts: anger, frustration, or being ignored. The infant learns that there are some parts of himself or herself that can't be expressed, because it threatens that secure relationship with the mother. This is the beginning of the False Self: dividing wishes, preferences, and impulses into acceptable and unacceptable categories, only showing the acceptable ones to the world, and forgetting that the unacceptable ones are still very much present.

Stop here for a moment and think about yourself. When you are in a new situation meeting people, *how do you introduce yourself?* Do you know who you really are?

The full flowering of my False Self came at Pasadena High School in 1960. At one of the premier high schools in America, with 4,200 students, I was the first tenth-grader chosen for the men's honorary service club, the Key Club. I enjoyed more affirmation in football, student government, and the inner circle of popularity, which culminated in my election as District Governor of all of the Key Clubs in California, Nevada, and Hawaii. I was so busy and involved that I needed a personal assistant! I still look back at those three years of high school wistfully. In April 1963 I pleased my parents immensely when I was accepted to the University of Southern California, the only school to which I had applied, where no fewer than seven of my aunts and uncles had attended. I had pleased the whole family. In June came even better news: I had been awarded a full scholarship!

However, the False Self has an insatiable appetite. At the senior awards assembly, plaques and trophies were given to outstanding scholars, student leaders, and athletes. At the announcement of each award, I was breathless in expectation. But there was no trophy for me. I remember slowly walking the hallway in the administration building after that event, staring blankly at display windows inside the building, my eyes welling up with tears and my throat choking. I lacked perspective. I had just received a scholarship that today would be worth $200,000, and there I was, blubbering because I did not get a $25 brass plaque!

At USC the days of reckoning descended on me. Trying to be the perfect, successful son had its price. My first love relationship challenged the attention of my parents, especially my mother. That relationship broke up because of my compulsive lying and other dysfunctions. I blamed my parents for my unhappiness and did not see them for many months, even though they lived just twenty miles away. The isolation was increasing. I stole books from the Doheny Library where I worked, and tried to sell them at a Pasadena bookstore. I was arrested on my twenty-first birthday. The university decided not to press charges but to dismiss me from the school.

The house of cards had collapsed. I was now a total failure, though, granted, I had not been slung in jail. Here was the beginning of what Dr. Bob would say was a glimpse of an unmanageable life. Fortunately, my uncle, John Trever, was able to get me into Baldwin Wallace College in Ohio, where I could finish my studies.

But here is the weird part: in the midst of isolation, anger and bad choices, I was attending the Episcopal church in Altadena, California. There I had found a new family-community that welcomed me, where I did not have to perform to meet what I thought were the expectations of others. I volunteered in the Sunday school, teaching an unruly class of second-graders, and I sang in the choir. I was being drawn toward the priesthood, as I deeply admired the parish priest and his social activism. I was encouraged to apply for seminary.

The discernment process for ordination involved a psychiatric exam and the doctor must have seen the turbulence within me. My application was denied. However, Uncle John, a Methodist minister, encouraged me to apply to the ecumenical religious school in Berkeley, California, the Pacific School of Religion. I was admitted. This was not the way things were done. You received your bishop's approval to attend seminary (always an Episcopal seminary) only after you were accepted to postulancy, the first step in the ordination process. I was behaving as a free agent, and that was extremely risky.

September 1967. The day I arrived at Berkeley, America's countercultural revolution was in full swing, and there I was at the center of it all. I rang the bell at the front door of the seminary and a student named Martin Murdock welcomed me. "I'm just heading out to a party. Want to come?"

"Yes."

Within the hour we had arrived at the corner of Haight and Ashbury, ground zero for San Francisco's Summer of Love. We went up two flights of stairs to a large apartment where some student nurses lived. We were welcomed to the strains of folk music and good times. What strikingly beautiful ladies were there! Then came the shock—one of many I experienced in three years of Berkeley student life: all of these beautiful student nurses had been nuns in the Los Angeles community of the Immaculate Heart of Mary. In the heated conflict with the old-time traditionalist Cardinal MacIntyre, following the hopes for liberalization engendered by the Second Vatican Council, the religious order was kicked out of Los Angeles and many of its nuns had left the community and come to the Bay Area. Most of the other young men I saw at the party turned out to be novices in the Order of Christian Brothers.

I return to Dr. Bob's couch, the panic attacks, and the False Self. The False Self is a fearful place to live. I had to be ever on the defensive. I needed constant approval. I wanted to please and to be a successful priest. I couldn't let anyone get too close, including Janice, my wife. I was in that lonely place, discerned by Basil Pennington:

> Down beneath all that we have and all that we do is that little one who is all need and is ever trying to win the approbation of others in the hope that it might ultimately assure us that we are worth something.[5]

This is what drives us to psychiatrists and emergency rooms where we can get pills to sedate us because we don't want to live with the pain of sleepless anxiety. I asked Dr. Bob for pills to calm me and to help me sleep. He said no. I needed to go through this cold turkey, and besides, with pills I would certainly become an addict. But he did offer Janice medication—because she had to live with me. She refused.

The wisdom people of the world religions tell us that the prescription for liberation from the False Self, from restless desire and endless

---

5. Pennington, *True Self/False Self*, 46.

dissatisfaction, is some form of meditation. This is actually what the Buddha tells us. In the Four Noble Truths he diagnosed the core spiritual problem of humanity: *duhkha*, the endlessly dissatisfying nature of life, which fame, sex, power, and money cannot answer. The Buddha's prescription for liberation is the Eightfold Path, with *sarsen*, sitting meditation, at the core.

Lao Tzu echoes this when he invites us to sit on a rock with him at the edge of the forest, watch the flowing ripples of the stream next to us, and empty our minds, quiet all that thinking and desire, and become one with the Great Mother of all things, the Tao.

Hindu sadhus invite us into the forest for meditation with yoga. As we harness our body and breath, the mind will be tamed, and we will flow into the deep place of Atman, intuitive consciousness, where we become one with God. Meditation helps us to simply *be*. The last struggle of the False Self is against our thinking.

Dr. Bob, the psychiatrist, was also a kind of spiritual director guiding me closer to the Holy One. The restlessness, panic attacks, and depression were clearly not psychological aberrations alone; they were also connected with a spiritual crisis.

Ron Rolheiser writes in *The Holy Longing*:

> . . . we are forever restless, dissatisfied, frustrated and aching. We are so overcharged with desire that it is hard to simply rest. . . . We are driven persons, forever obsessed, congenitally dis-eased, living lives of quiet desperation.[6]

There is a fire that burns within us, a wild desire pulling us this way and that way. Rolheiser continues:

> Spirituality is . . . about what we do with that desire. What we do with our longings. . . . Thus when Plato says that we are on fire because our souls come from beyond and that beyond is, through the longing and hope that its fire creates in us, trying to draw us back toward itself, he is laying out the broad outlines for spirituality. Likewise, for Augustine, when he says, "You have made us for yourself. Lord, our hearts are restless until they rest in you." Spirituality is about what we do with our unrest.[7]

Spirituality is about what we do with our sleepless Saturday nights when the panic attacks hit. I know what Rolheiser means by the fire that

---

6. Rolheiser, *Holy Longing*, 3.

7. Ibid., 5.

burns within, and I think you do too. You know restless dissatisfaction. You have had your nights of tossing and turning. Rolheiser has a wonderful sentence in *The Holy Longing* that is especially good for priests to hear: "Spirituality is more about whether or not we can sleep at night than about whether or not we go to church."[8] It has something to do with how I live with this fire inside me and how I channel my eros and the disciplines and habits of my life. Will these energies take me in all directions, chasing satiation of the appetites of the False Self, or will the fire take me deep within, to that God-shaped void that only the Holy One can fill?

I also found sustenance and guidance at the Center for Spiritual Development in Orange, California. This ecumenical center is open to all spiritualities and provides spiritual directors who are trained in helping us listen within, and to connect in deep friendship with the Holy One. It was here that I learned about meditation and centering prayer. The Spiritual Exercises of Saint Ignatius of Loyola, a five hundred-year-old curriculum for praying through the Gospels and the life of Jesus, brought me deeper into communion with God. We need wise teachers who point the way and remind us that we are beloved by God. This is where I was given the tools and disciplines that have helped me for over twenty years.

It has been a very long pilgrimage for me, leading me home to that for which I was created: communion with the Holy One. For more than twenty years, the desert has become that place where I am most able to quiet my mind and enter into love, joy, peace, and hope with God.

And then, in forty years of marriage and of being a parent, I began to meet my True Self in the love I have received from Janice, Erik, and Katie. As a continuously flawed human, with all sorts of odd conditions in my psychic makeup, they each have loved me. Remembering that I have been loved by others in spite of myself is a great joy. Basil Pennington reveals, "The only way we really see ourselves is when we see ourselves reflected back to us from the eyes of one who truly loves us."[9] Ultimately that person is God. I find my True Self in communion with the Holy One.

A daily practice of meditation guides us toward the True Self. Let me share with you such a practice that has helped me. It is called the Examen of Consciousness and it was developed by Ignatius Loyola five hundred years ago. There are a few easy steps, and this is how I practice them.

8. Ibid., 7.

9. Quoted from Hernandez, *Henri Nouwen and Spiritual Polarities*, ch. 1.

At the end of my day, there is a goodnight kiss for Jan and a hug for our son, Erik (who sleeps in a bed about six feet from ours, because of his night seizures). When all is quiet, I gaze up into the dark ceiling and reflect on the day. I begin by inviting God to be present with me.

Gratitude: I try to recall the good things that happened during the day, the little blessings for which I want to give thanks. I am not doing a self-assessment here, or a fantasy trip through the day that is past; rather, I want to anchor myself in the place of thanksgiving. Perhaps there is good news, or an enjoyable family experience, or an encounter with God in creation that bubbles up. Some of these experiences can be powerful and I want to savor them rather than rush through a vague memory and brush it aside. Savoring an experience for which I am thankful slows down the whole experience and I am blessed by that event.

I ask for the grace to see where I have turned away from my True Self, the deepest part of myself. I allow myself to see those times when I was not at my best. Maybe I was hard on someone, insensitive. The point is not to beat up on myself, but to let the voice of my conscience remind me of a better way. Maybe tomorrow I need to go back to that person to make amends. As I pay attention to this voice of conscience, God is helping me to be more loving.

I review the day as though I am watching a video. I begin from the moment I awoke and go through every event. I pay attention to what made me happy, what helped me relax when I felt stressed, confused, frustrated. I try to recreate with all my senses the past day. The surprise is that when you make this a daily practice you find that events and people otherwise forgotten often have something very important connected to them.

I ask God to pardon what I may have done that was not loving.

I resolve with God's grace to make amends where I can. I ask for God's help in the coming day.

I close with a prayer.

During the night (when I have to make those middle-aged male visits to the bathroom) I am sometimes astonished by moments of great clarity. A phrase comes forth in answer to a problem I have been praying about. Regular meditation opens the mind's filters to the flow of intuitive consciousness. Some of my most creative ideas or answers to conflict have come from these 3 a.m. Aha!s.

Lest you think that this is my own private hobby, a linear project of self-perfection, you should know that my favorite mystic, Thomas Merton, wrestled all of his life with his own cunning False Self. You can read about these struggles in his journals and letters. As a maturing mystic of the Trappist Cistercian order, the new project of his False Self was to become the perfect monk. Some of his earliest writings expressed his project-oriented spirituality and his image of the perfect monk. However, meditation in the presence of God's love revealed to him the truth of his wanderings, and he wrote about it in *New Seeds of Contemplation*:

> For me to become a saint means to be myself. Therefore, the problem of sanctity and salvation is in fact the problem of finding out who I am and of discovering my True Self. The recognition of the True Self in the divine image is recognition of the fact that we are known and loved by God.[10]

And lest you think the False Self has been fully exorcised in me, sociologist Erving Goffman reminds us that all of life is performance and we act out using different personae depending on whom we are with and the context.

There is a reason why most of the wisdom people who helped birth the major world religions had their foundational experience of the Holy in the desert. The desert reveals and fosters the True Self. Spindly creosote branches brush against my jeans and a sweet sage-scented autumn breeze caresses me as I walk in the morning light. My soul becomes like an old bed sheet strung up between two pine trees. The gentle wind of the Spirit blows through me. This is my favorite mediation, the yoga that quiets body and breath and mind, walking in the vast spaces of the Owens Valley, where I embrace my True Self.

I hope that you may try some of the desert paths for yourself. Perhaps you will stay in Lone Pine, at the Dow Villa Motel, in room 20. At the end of the day, your muscles will feel tired but well spent. Perhaps there you may practice the Examen of Consciousness, discovering a surprising wellspring of deep thanksgiving for the graces of creation, the beloved people in your life, and for the renewed awareness that you are precious to the Holy One. Just before you turn off the lamp in the room, a portrait of the Duke himself will gaze upon you as a final blessing. Tonight you will sleep very well.

10. Merton, *New Seeds of Contemplation*, 31.

10

Encounters with Native American Spirituality and a Meditation Walk to the Site of a Paiute Village

I never felt alone or afraid up there in the hills. The mmah-hah stories described the conversations coyotes, crows and buzzards used to have with human beings. I was fascinated with the notion that long ago humans and animals used to freely converse. As I got older, I realized the clouds and winds and rivers also have their ways of communication; I became interested in what these entities had to say. My imagination became engaged in discovering what can be known without words.

—LESLIE MARMON SILKO[1]

An Indian needs to speak with God, and so, obedient to his Christian training, he travels to the Vatican, where the Pope has a red phone, a hotline to God. But the Indian can't talk at length because it's a long-distance call. The next time the Indian needs to speak with God, he remembers his disappointment and decides to drop by the tribal medicine man's house. Turns out the medicine man has a hotline to God. On that phone, however, the Indian can talk as long as he wants because it is a local call.

—MICHAEL JOHNSON[2]

1. Silko, *Turquoise Ledge*, 45.
2. Johnson, *Hunger for the Wild*, 18.

JUNE 24, 1984. WE were spiritual tourists at the Taos Pueblo, high in the mountains of northern New Mexico. The searing rays of summer drove us into the shelter of Saint Jerome Chapel. Janice, my wife, held one-year-old Erik in her arms as his eight-year-old sister, Katie, drew close. We leaned against the cool adobe walls and sighed with relief. The San Juan Day Corn Dance was supposed to begin at five that afternoon but it seemed to be running late. I asked one of the reservation security people when the dance would begin. "Hard to say," he replied. "We are on Indian time here." Another tourist chuckled, as if this answer indicated a woefully lax attitude on the part the natives. But I was thinking otherwise: *sacred time is all about the right time.*

I am gazing across the plaza at two clusters of multistoried adobe pueblos. Long wooden ladders connect each level. A stream filled with clear, bubbling water flows between the two massive structures. The water is from the sacred Blue Lake high in the mountains to the northeast. One hundred and fifty Tiwa now live in this settlement that has stood for a thousand years. They choose a traditional lifestyle: no electricity or piped water.

An ancient man clad in a red robe climbs a wooden ladder to the roof of the third level of the pueblo. His worn but strong voice crackles and rises in volume and intensity. To whom is he shouting? He thrusts both arms up towards the sun, continuing his shouting in a rhythmic cadence.I see a drum at the corner of one of the dwellings. It is a good six feet in diameter and surrounded by five men beating a hypnotic rhythm. A cloud of dust billows towards them and then the dancers emerge in two rows. One is of young women shaking maracas and holding aloft ears of corn. Cornhusks hang from their waistbands. The other row is of young bare-chested men, some with eagle feathers in their hair. The dancers move together with measured hops, the drum beats faster.

I watch, wondering if this interaction of corn and young men and women is connected with the fertility of the corn crop. Behind me, another tourist begins a commentary to his group, explaining what he sees. "See that dancer wearing the red sash? This is an authentic corn dance . . ." I try to listen to glean information, and then something catches me and pulls me back. There is a tightening of my stomach in resistance. I look back at the dancers and sigh as I see their faces. This is *prayer*, not some floor show. These people are praying! And now I think about the time of Holy Communion in my church. The priest moving down the Communion rail, holding up the host while saying, "Body of Christ, Bread of Heaven," and placing it with reverence in an open hand. I imagine that same irritating guy somewhere in the shadows, saying, "See that priest over there? This is an authentic Mass! Let me explain it to you . . ." No, the weaving, undulating lines of young men and women are not part of a tourist-trap performance; I am watching people at prayer. And I begin to pray with them.

Paiute grinding stones near Independence Creek, 2014. Author's collection.

Over the last two hundred years, the Pueblo Indians have become more and more secretive about their rituals. This is because American and European anthropologists have camped out on the reservations, seduced the people with gifts, developed and betrayed relationships, and made bank from the sacred secrets. The tribal mysteries appeared in print and made a name for the scholars, but an essential part of the rituals was compromised. As a result, the Pueblo people do not now share information about rituals—even with a spouse, if he or she is of a different clan.

The Swiss psychoanalyst Carl Jung visited the Taos Pueblo in the 1930s, while working on his exploration of myth and ritual among world cultures. One day he was up on that same roof as the ancient man in the red robe. There, as the summer sun hovered overhead, the Pueblo chief, Och-wiay Biano, spoke with Jung: "Is not he who moves there our father? How can anyone say differently? How can there be another god? Nothing can be without the sun." Jung noticed a building excitement within the Pueblo holy man, as he struggled to express the ineffable. "What would a man do alone in the mountains? He cannot even build his fire without him."

Jung asked the chief whether the sun might actually be a creation of God. The holy man brushed off the question, replying, "The sun *is* God. Everyone can see that."

Jung continued his probing: "You think, then, what you do in your religion benefits the whole world?"

The shaman replied: "Of course. If we did not do it, what would become of the world? We are a people who live on the roof of the world; we are the sons of Father Sun, and with our religion, we daily help our Father go across the sky. We do this not only for ourselves, but also for the whole world. If we were to cease practicing our religion, in ten years the sun would no longer rise. Then it would be night forever."

Jung pondered this "naïve" response, and gave us this insightful reflection:

> I then realized on what the "dignity," the tranquil composure of
> the individual Indian, was founded. It springs from his being a son
> of the sun; his life is cosmologically meaningful, for he helps the
> father and preserver of all life in his daily rise and descent. If we
> set against this our own self-justifications, the meaning of our own
> lives as it is formulated by our reason, we are obliged to smile at
> the Indians' naïveté and to plume ourselves on our cleverness; for

otherwise we would discover how impoverished and down at the heels we are. Knowledge does not enrich us; it removes us more and more from the mythic world in which we were once at home by right of birth.[3]

Are we spiritually homeless, as Jung suggests? What is the attraction of Native American spirituality to you? As you read about the sense of coexistence between humans and the natural world, and cozy encounters with earth creatures, is there a yearning beyond words that stirs within you?

As inheritors of European rationalism, most Americans live in a culture that is suspicious of mystery and enchantment. One definition of religion is, "That which connects all of life together." To take one example, there was a time when the great city of Paris, France, lived this definition holistically. In the late medieval period, religion was the warp and weft of the fabric of society: the monarchy, the courts, the guilds, the villages, the social resources, the calendar, the schools and university, hospitals and medicine, the inns and roads, and even the marketplace were all sustained by and tributary to the Roman Catholic Church. The Jew and the Muslim were not part of this cloth.

In his book *A Secular Age*, Charles Taylor draws a remarkable contrast between the year 1500 CE and our present age. In 1500 it was assumed that everyone believed in God. The natural world of storms, plagues, and floods were seen as divine activity. Daily life was interconnected with religious ritual and people lived in a world of spiritual enchantment. In the precariousness of the conflict between darkness and light, only those who were faithful believers lived in a secure place.

The kind of spiritual world we encounter today among practitioners of traditional indigenous religions, such as the Owens Valley Paiute, is very similar to the enchanted world of late medieval Europe. Then the world was filled with spiritual forces to be reckoned with. There was holy help from the saints and spiritual objects such as the Communion wafer of the Mass, holy water, anointing oil, and candles. And the landscape was of natural holy places such as springs, rivers, and mountain tops, each affording spiritual protection. However, if we were not careful, the power of the spirit world could possess us in terrible ways that might be manifested in sickness or madness or death. Paris in 1500 was enchanted: the spiritual world always had to be addressed, appeased, mollified. In this world, the Bible in Latin was the literal Word of God as interpreted by the Church,

3. Jung, *Memories, Dreams, Reflections*, 252.

which gave instruction particularly in how to negotiate the spiritual world and how to avoid its demons.

But during the following 150 years this perspective radically changed. Early scientists, among them Galileo and Francis Bacon, demanded that we use our human reason inductively by studying not the Bible but the Book of Nature. The French-Dutch mathematician René Descartes (1596–1650) is the philosopher we most identify as directing the shift from the old religious orthodoxy, where everyone was assumed to believe in God, to a new world, launching the modern age and the primacy of the individual. Descartes craved certainty. He began by putting aside all dogmatic assumptions about truth and turned to making a system of what the mind alone could know. One night, sitting in front of a fireplace in deep contemplation, what came to him was the one thing of which he could be certain: *Cogito ergo sum*, "I am thinking right here in this rocking chair in front of this fireplace, and therefore I do exist." At the basis of the new system, therefore, Descartes had to distinguish the mind from the body. The task of the mind is to control the body and its passions. The body is a machine that can be studied by the mind. Whereas tradition held that sickness had a spiritual cause, if we can study the body thoroughly we can find ways to heal sickness.

So began the disenchantment of the modern world. There would be no longer value in any mystical communion with nature or the cosmos. The new modern order required rational control. Descartes said that our best defense against falling back into the old superstitions was a "buffered self." Again, Charles Taylor writes:

> The buffered self is the agent who no longer fears demons, spirits and magic forces. More radically, these no longer impinge; they don't exist for him; whatever threat or other meaning they proffer doesn't "get it" from him.
>
> This super buffered self . . . is not only not "got at" by demons and spirits; he is also utterly unmoved by the aura of desire. In a mechanistic universe, and in a field of functionally understood passion, there is no more room for such an aura. There is nothing it could correspond to. It is just a disturbing, supercharged feeling, which somehow grips us until we can come to our senses, and take on our full, buffered identity.[4]

So, religion in Europe shifts from assumed affiliation to a prescribed spirit world to a personal decision one makes in life to abjure or ignore

---

4. Taylor, *Secular Age*, 135.

or disengage from the mystical. Spiritual experiences of the enchantment within nature are shunted off into an isolated corner. In such a social construct, real knowledge and progress can come only through the application of human reason.

Another important factor in the loss of our religious innocence was the Protestant Reformation of the mid-sixteenth century. In 1905 the German sociologist Max Weber, in *The Protestant Ethic and the Rise of Capitalism*, described how, by denying the sacramental and dismissing all magic and enchantment as the work of the devil, and by connecting the work ethic to commercial success, the Protestant Reformation opened the way for antireligious humanism.

A third driver of the disenchantment of the West occurred in North America. At one time the thirteen colonies each had their own state church. For example, if you lived in the colony of Virginia, you would be assumed to be Anglican. But with the efforts of Jefferson and Madison applying the new teachings of the Age of Reason, the American Constitution endorsed the radical idea that every person should be free to choose his or her own spiritual path. This meant that inhabitants of the nascent United States would not be compelled to give allegiance to a religion in which they did not believe.

Owens Valley Paiute woman at grinding stone, ca. 1890.
County of Inyo, Eastern California Museum.

Robert Bellah, in his classic study of American life, *Habits of the Heart*, charts the progress of religion in America and shows how we moved from established state churches, to which in colonial times we were compelled to belong, to a disestablished spirituality. Thus, religion became a private matter in the constitutional United States.

Recently, however, something has been happening in the United States that suggests a contrary trend. Since the late 1960s, there has been a New Great Awakening. Immigrants from Asia brought with them strong traditions of Buddhism, Taoism, and Hinduism, which fostered and nurtured explorations of personal religious experiences among the secularized people of the United States. It was not long before this new spiritual searching embraced Native American spirituality, in which it was recognized that there is an antidote to the cold, rational, buffered self of the secular age.

Father Paul Steinmetz is a Jesuit priest who has spent his life in ministry with the Lakota Sioux. He shares this insight:

> Native American Spirituality is a part of Technological Man, a part of himself which he has repressed into his unconscious. It is for this reason that Native Americans can help Technological Man get in touch with his own primal roots. This is the only way he will redeem the world of nature, which he has been exploiting and polluting. No program or plan will accomplish this. It must be a spirituality that expresses a personal relationship with nature, a willingness not to dominate but to be a part of nature and an ability to view creation sacramentally. But Technological Man must not only bring up this spirituality from his primal unconscious, he must also assimilate the contents into his own conscious life, a process Carl Jung called individuation.[5]

5. Steinmetz, *Meditations with the Lakota*, preface.

Traditional Paiute dwelling, ca. 1900. County of Inyo, Eastern California Museum.

As you walk with me in the Owens Valley, you enter a land in which, for more than ten thousand years, traditional religion has lived a relationship with the visible world and the world of spirit. Humans share kinship with all creatures of the natural world and with the world of spirit. Because creation is in a constant state of flux and deconstruction, rituals and ceremonies are used in the work of achieving and maintaining harmony and balance, forestalling disintegration. Animals such as the fox, coyote, snake, and hawk are often intermediaries between humans and the spirit world; they are the important links. Men and women who have been touched in a special way by the spirits become shamans, powerful healers who are able to penetrate the "thin places" between humans in the visible world and the spirit world. For the shaman, the religious specialist, powers and visions are a matter of direct experience. There is a common view of the cycle of life and death and of cosmic harmony. The world of the traditional Native American is a numinous world in which all activity is spiritual.

Traveling north past the intersection of Highways 14 and 395, the road hugs the western shoulder of a vast ancient lakebed known today as Indian

Wells Valley. In the distance, you see a narrow notch between the Sierra and Argus ranges. Through this gap once flowed glacial waters that spilled around where you are now, and eastward, to fill the basins of Panamint Valley and Death Valley. As the road climbs to pass through the gap, high cliffs of volcanic reefs loom up toward you from the east. Suddenly, the green-blue waters of Little Lake appear on your right, the land flattens, and a huge red hill thrusts into view. You have entered the land of the Numa People, the Owens Valley Paiute. Six tribes claim this valley: Panamint, Lone Pine, Independence, Big Pine, Bishop, and Benton are now their reservations. Driving north on 395, you pass through quiet desert settlements each with a distinctive sign of the local tribe posted at the town limits.

For ten thousand years, family clusters lived in a verdant land of dashing deer, gushing blue waters, and clouds of wildfowl. But in the mid-1800s this primal Eden suddenly changed with the incursions of European American explorers and mountain men, the discovery of gold and silver in the Inyo Mountains, the settlement of towns, and the introduction of the cattle and sheep that sustained the invasion. As the native people frantically defended their villages and food sources, conflict intensified. The US Calvary from Fort Independence rounded up the tribes and marched them on their own Trail of Tears southward to Fort Tehachapi. Many died in that forced march, though some were able to escape. Eventually the survivors, deprived of their lands and way of life, would be compelled to find work as washerwomen, house servants, farm workers and cowboys.

One hundred and fifty years later, Paiute life has shifted back into self-determination. Profits from the popular Paiute Casino in Bishop and shared income from other casinos have resulted in new homes, jobs, community health clinics, early childhood education centers, and progressive programs for addiction recovery and the prevention of domestic violence. New generations of Paiutes are returning to the reservation as teachers, attorneys, and community organizers. For all this change, their spiritual connection to the land and the traditional religion continues.

Let us take the opportunity for a meditative walk through this enchanted land. First we will go to a local museum for orientation. A drive of fifteen minutes north from Lone Pine, on Highway 395, brings us to the town of Independence. Look for the post office on the left. Turn west on Market Street, heading toward the Sierra Nevada. This road would eventually bring you to Onion Valley, the base camp to hike up over Kearsarge

Pass, but today, after a few blocks, turn right at Grant Street, which will take you to the Eastern California Museum.

In the parking lot you will find a display of antique mining tools and farm equipment. There are also buildings that have been moved here from local ghost towns. The museum itself is a gem and will help you get a feel for the complex, multicultural history of the Owens Valley. There is an extensive bookstore. The displays tell the stories of the Manzanar World War II Japanese American Relocation Camp, the development of mining, and how the area has been farmed. A rare collection of Native American basketwork is located in a separate wing of the museum. You will want to return to this Native American section after your walk.

Walking north from the museum building, we come to the Mary DeDecker Native Plant Garden and Nature Trail. In 2001, volunteers from the Bristlecone chapter of the California Native Plant Society planted forty-three species here, representing eighteen plant families, including saltbrush, desert olive, water birch, and western hackberry. The garden includes several well-placed benches that invite contemplation. I sit down and bask in the spring sunshine. Water from Independence Creek flows around me and the desert landscape spills westward, leading to the snow-blanketed Sierra Nevada. As the sun warms me, I am so grateful to God for the glory of creation that I can feel it: prickly shivers course through my body. It is hard to slow down my busy mind, even out here in the tranquility and loveliness of nature. I am thinking about exploring, photographing, evaluating, studying, and writing down what I see and all my reactions. But gradually, as I sit on this bench, surrounded by astounding splendor, God becomes very close. My mind stills. Thoughts come and evaporate. I breathe in calm and I am grateful.

It is a sunny March morning. I take the sinuous trail. The spicy perfume of sagebrush (*Artesmisia tridentate*) fills the air. Two bridges made of railroad ties take me over Independence Creek. Soft wind blows down from Kearsarge Pass, music of water washing over rocks and birds singing. I continue on the trail through an opening in a barbed-wire fence.

Suddenly I am captivated by a surprising sight. All around me are the tiniest of spring flowers in full bloom. Last week six inches of snow covered the ground and today delicate miniature yellow, blue, and red flowers line the trail. And here is another surprise: a shallow, flat rock holding five grinding holes. Here is where Paiute/Numa women once prepared food. Seventy percent of their food came from vegetation such as lovegrass, blue dicks, tomcat clover, yellow nut-grass, and Indian mountain grass. The extended family clusters would continuously gather their food from the land, which accounts for much of their extensive migration.

I follow the trail heading to another branch of Independence Creek. As I come to the trailhead, I turn to circle back to the museum, and another surprise: more grinding stones. These are a rare sight in my usual desert hikes, but here there are dozens! This is indicative of a substantial village with its domed *toni nobe* circular shelters made from willow and tule reeds. The willow branches were woven to make a frame, which would be covered with tule bundles. A single door in each faced the sunrise. I can even see some circles of stone, which may well be foundations for the toni nobe. Standing among the remains of this village, I see the grinding holes and mortar pestles being used. I hear the rhythmic sounds of pounding and grinding, and the chatter of the grandmothers, mothers, and daughters together. There is singing. This is home. Sanctuary.

Belden Lane writes:

> Such quaint naïveté seems absurd to the modern mind. . . . Large dimensions of our humanity are denied by the very loss of what Native Americans have sought all along to maintain. A sense of transcendence, a love of the earth, a renewed vision, a story worth telling, silence in the presence of mystery—all these are aspects of the American Indian quest for a fuller humanity. The reductionist attempt to discount such ideas as lingering vestiges of a pre-scientific age may ultimately endanger our own survival.[6]

6. Lane, *Landscapes of the Sacred*, 92.

11

Finding Gratitude in the Desert

Gratitude is the foundation of future hope. Hope without gratitude is wishful thinking.

—Father Gordon Moreland, SJ[1]

For Augustine, human memories are the most powerful dynamisms in a person's life precisely because they are not merely frozen snapshots of the past pasted in some wilting picture album. Rather, they are the dynamic and present recall of past events.

—David Hassel, SJ[2]

The desert helps us to remember who we are and Who it is that loves us.

Twenty miles south of Lone Pine, the remains of the village of Olancha appear as an atoll in a sagebrush ocean. One hundred and fifty years ago, this was a stagecoach stop on the way to the gold and silver mines in the Inyo Mountains. Ruins of old adobes and the main street stores stand roofless, walls tumbling, painted with fading advertisements for 1930s beer and groceries. The approach is lined with ninety-foot cottonwood trees standing sentry, resplendent with shimmering, golden autumn. Their leaves flutter and fall around me: nature's tickertape welcome.

1. Moreland said this during a spiritual direction session on April 16, 2013, at the House of Prayer, in Orange, CA.
2. Hassel, *Prayer of Reminiscence*, 3.

Look for Fall Road as you enter Olancha from the south; it is after the gas station on your left. If you come to School Road, you have gone too far. As you drive west on Fall Road with the Sierra Nevada before you, you will come to the bed of a spur of the Southern Pacific Railroad, the rails of which were removed in about 2002. The paved road turns sharply left to a talcum plant. Turn your car around here and park near the neighboring homes. Walk back over the ghost railroad and the bridge that crosses the Los Angeles Aqueduct. You will see a dirt road heading directly west towards the Sierra Nevada. Several trails fan out at this point.

When I walk in this area, I focus my attention on one of the creeks flowing down from the mountains. They are delineated by rows of trees. Walker Creek and Olancha Creek (where Crystal Geyser bottled water comes from) are my favorite targets for meditative walks through this wide open landscape.

For forty years, the autumn season held mixed blessings for me as a parish priest. On the one hand, football season returned. Go USC Trojans! Go Pasadena High School Bulldogs! On the other, it was the season of greatest anxiety for me. Autumn is stewardship time, when churches and synagogues launch their fundraising campaigns for the forthcoming year. For forty years, I entered this season with an apprehension that amounted to real fear. Will there be enough money next year to fund the program staff and ministries? One way I used this fearful energy was in obsessively formulating plans for marketing, promotion, and solicitation. In 1981, when I became pastor at Messiah Episcopal Parish, our annual budget was $50,000. When I retired in 2011, our pledges were over ten times that amount. We used many of the fundraising techniques developed by secular non-profit organizations. In terms of cash, (at the least) the parish became very successful. In fact the Diocese of Los Angeles published our solicitation program as a national model! Nonetheless, I was always very anxious about coming up short in the fundraising. My time walking out here in the rocky landscape around Olancha changed me and brought me to another place: a place of remembrance and gratitude. I learned that beyond MBA-inspired fundraising programs, God wanted me to help parishioners to remember their personal encounters with Amazing Grace in the crises of their lives. In remembering, gratitude to God would flow in their hearts and they could be moved to generosity. This is not to say, of course, that emphasizing the virtue of gratitude to God was intended to swell the parish coffers!

For forty years the Hebrew people wandered in the desert wilderness of Sinai. That was long enough for most of the generation that was born into slavery in Egypt to die off. Even Moses himself would not enter the Lands of Promise. But see how in that desert space over those years, the Chosen People became entirely dependent on God. We read in the Book of Exodus about their foundational story of salvation in the desert, which, the prophets always preached, had to be remembered. In that empty place, God provided manna, a strange sustaining substance secreted by desert plants. Manna could not be stored. If you tried, it would either melt in the sun or be consumed by worms. The Lord God only provided enough manna for one day. Thus, in the place of desolation, the people learned absolute dependence on God's Amazing Grace.

And when the Chosen finally arrived at a point where they could spy the verdant Jordan River Valley in the distance, Moses gave his farewell sermon. He warned that though abundance appeared on the horizon, the Israelites should not forget what God had done for them out there in the wilderness. Only so long as they remembered this would God continue to bless them.

I am walking on a trail towards Olancha Creek on the second day of a four-day retreat. My busy thoughts are beginning to slow down and my senses are alert. The crunching sands and large boulders around me are the results of thousands of years of wind, flood, and erosion. It is a slow climb, heart beating, breathing more intense. Listen. As I walk uphill along Olancha Creek, I see no water flowing, but I do hear it. Cottonwood and willow trees rustle gently in the cool wind. I climb over a rise of boulders and suddenly see where the spring is flowing into the creek. Somewhere behind me it disappears into the gravelly soil, but here water rushes over boulders and sagebrush. For centuries, this was a place for Paiute ceremonies, vision quests, and shamanic retreats. I hear the wind, the bubbling water, and the crunching sands. A red-tailed hawk shrieks above me. Memories begin to seep into my blissfully emptied head.

Different interior voices can speak to us. When we are not walking with the Holy Presence we are vulnerable to that insistent voice that you and I recognize all too well: the Critic. Memories of a recent argument or disappointment become vivid and seethe. Feelings begin to boil. Negative, critical thoughts seep into even this most tranquil of settings. Memories of how I have disappointed or hurt people in the deeper past rear their ugly heads. This flood and turmoil of guilty recollection can drag me down into despair. Saint Ignatius called this phenomenon "encounters with the dark spirits." His forebear, Saint Augustine, remind us that our memories are not just fixed pictures of our past but that they continue to have a dynamic and powerful influence on us. I walk, and these baleful memories do bubble up like a fetid, poison spring. The most important thing I can do now is to invite the Lord to be with me here alongside Olancha Creek.

I walk among murmuring trees, water gurgling in a creek, and memories ebb and flow in my mind. This is what Father David Hassle calls the Prayer of Personal Reminiscence. He describes this as "Reliving one's memories with Christ present so that the praying person can repossess his or her life in a more maturely Christian way."[3] Left alone with some of my memories, my poor decisions, and the hurt I have caused does haunt me. For instance, when I was expelled from the University of Southern California in 1966, it seemed like the end of my academic career, and I know I was a huge disappointment to my parents. However, as I look back at that failure through the eyes of Christ, I can see how God was awakening me to my self-deception and denial. A turn in the road led me to another college, where, like the people of the desert exodus, my life was stripped of entitlements and I became dependent solely on God's Amazing Grace. This led me deeper into my life with God, toward seminary and the priesthood.

I spend most of the day around this rocky, riparian landscape, memories flowing in and out of my mind. The ever active Critic resurfaces. Yet because I know I am loved and blessed by the Holy Presence, I can look pretty squarely at my painful memories. I can delve into those secret places where I am most vulnerable. As I review my life with the light of the Holy Presence, I am liberated from building ever stouter defenses, the stultifying mental blocks and self-destructive thoughts.

The stark beauty of the desert in autumn takes my breath away. I ask the Lord to guide my understanding of these memories and how this understanding can help me serve God as a more compassionate, grateful person.

Understanding comes like the wind and surprises me. My heart wells up with deep gratitude to God as memory opens up in great clarity, I recollect all the times when though I was at the end of my tether, running on empty, and the Lord brought me through the wilderness to blessings, joy, peace, love, and hope.

After several hours of walking, I can see from nature's clock that it is time to return to my car. The sun sets early here, behind the Sierra Nevada. When I get back I see from the dashboard clock that I have been hiking

3. Ibid., 5.

with God for five hours. Driving back to the Dow Villa Motel in Lone Pine, where I frequently stay, I have a powerful sense of heightened alertness to the Spirit and indeed for other lost memories that might be lifted into my consciousness. In the motel room, I write in my journal a summary of my experience and what I heard the Lord saying to me by the creek.

Memories of such encounters with the Holy become foundational in our lives. They are touchstones that become keepsakes. We can return to them to help us remember that we are beloved of God and that all will be well. Not only this, but accompanying the Holy One in the wilderness pulls our hearts to true gratitude.

I mentioned above Father Gordon Moreland of the Society of Jesus; he is my spiritual director. He recently said this to me: "Gratitude is the foundation of future hope. Hope without gratitude is wishful thinking." What that says to me is that those vivid times when God's Amazing Grace has been with me, and I have really known it, underpin me as I step into the future in hope: a hope, a certainty that, like the Israelites, God will sustain me for another day. If I have no gratitude to God for astonishing blessings and for God's presence with me in the past, then all I have is a lonely walk, all I have is wishful thinking, hoping for the best and not really believing that the best is for me.

The desert helps us to remember who we are and Who it is that loves us.

12

Remembering Manzanar

All things whatsoever which deserve to be dreaded and revered for the extraordinary and preeminent powers which they possess, are called the Kami.

—NORINAGA, EIGHTEENTH-CENTURY SHINTO SCHOLAR[1]

There's a belief that people die twice. Once, when you die, and once when you're forgotten—when people stop talking about you and they forget about you.

—RUDY CORDOVA[2]

LIKE A MIST OF sifting powdered sugar, the cloudbank of snow moves rapidly toward me from the Sierra Nevada in the west. I walk a deeply sanded road on the edge of Manzanar, the World War II relocation camp for Japanese Americans, on Highway 395, nine miles north of Lone Pine. More than sixty years after the closing of the camp, I can clearly see the foundations of the tightly packed barracks that housed ten thousand people in this harsh desert.

The wind blows hard as the snow envelops me, stinging my cheeks with the cold slap of winter. I have to get out of this wind! I turn up the collar of my heavy Carhartt jacket, pull the black fur Stetson hat tight upon my head, and walk into a dense thicket of trees. The thick overgrown foliage is nature's way of balancing the blow of the snow. I sit on the three-foot-diameter corpse of a fallen cottonwood to catch my breath. Boy, it is cold!

---

1. Quoted from Aston, *Shinto*, 6.
2. Quoted in "Day of the Dead," *Orange County Register*, November 1, 2012.

I gaze at the winter woods and see old apple and pear trees smothered by the new growth of desert willow and cottonwood. The fruit trees are survivors of the verdant orchards of the Manzanar of the early 1900s, before Los Angeles began to siphon off the precious Sierra snowmelt into its aqueduct. With a cracking snap I break off a scraping branch of cottonwood. It looks like dead wood, but I know these trees will be green again in June. The trees have walled off the wind and snow. I am catching my breath, but I am going to have to spend some time here.

Did you hear that? There is movement in the woods. The crunching of branches. I am not alone . . . Wind filters through the tightly woven strands of the barren trees, sighing. Sighing. This land has a heaviness. Echoes of displacement. Spirits moving about like hungry ghosts with no one to remember them.

Many of my Japanese-American high school classmates in Pasadena were babies or infants when they were wrenched from comfortable homes and brought to this benighted place, where the fine alkaline sand could not be kept out of the barrack housing and this same sighing wind pressed against thin wooden walls and lifted flimsy roof shingles.

In her memoir *Farewell to Manzanar*, Jeanne Wakasuki Houston remembers the day when her family was rounded up in the then middle-class suburbia of Boyle Heights, made to board buses at the Buddhist church in Los Angeles, and driven all day to the new Manzanar Camp:

> By the time we reached our destination . . . it was late afternoon. The first thing I saw was a yellow swirl across a blurred, reddish setting sun. The bus was being pelted by what sounded like splattering rain. It wasn't rain. This was my first look at something I would soon know very well, a billowing flurry of dust and sand churned up by the wind through Owens Valley. We drove past a barbed-wire fence, through a gate, and into an open space where trunks and sacks and packages had been dumped from the baggage trucks ahead of us. I could see a few tents set up, the first row of black barracks, and beyond them, blurred by sand, rows of barracks that seemed to spread for miles across this plain.[3]

As a result of the persecution, my classmates' families lost businesses, homes, and community roots. For four years, they struggled to re-establish their lives in compressed, enforced community, behind barbed wire and guard towers with machine guns. When you visit Manzanar today, you

---

3. Wakasuki and Houston, *Farewell to Manzanar*, 18.

enter through the old community hall, which is now a visitor's center and museum. You walk through a mockup barrack residence and can get a feel for life as it was. Every time I do this, what catches my heart is the cry of an infant. I look around at the other visitors and I am sure there must be some mother with a little one, crying for attention. But no, this is a recording of a baby crying, part of the exhibition. I imagine a young mother trying to nurse her baby as the snow pelts the tiny windows and seeps through the wooden wall slats.

The crying of the infant brings me back to another time: June 16, 1983. Our newborn son, Erik, was being held by my wife as she sat in our living room visiting with her mother, Evelyn. The picture of composed domesticity. Then something happened. There was a slight tremor through Erik's body. Jan had fifteen years of emergency room nursing experience and her instincts were aroused. Another very slight tremor. Erik was having seizures. The ten-pound healthy boy was in trouble. By the next day we were in PedICU at the Children's Hospital of Orange County. Jan had been up all night, and when I arrived I saw an intravenous drip connected to a vein in our baby's bald head. Erik had encephalitis; his brain was on fire and it hurt. When he woke up he cried the cry of one in real pain. Any parent hearing this would find it unbearable. Jan and I hung together through a week in the hospital. Erik recovered and came home with minimal discernible aftereffects, except, as we learned four years later, the medical school resident had failed to perform a simple routine test called a TORCH screen. That would have told us the viral cause of the meningitis. Exactly four years later, June 16, 1987, Erik's little brain would catch fire once more and our lives would change forever.

I hear the sound of crying again as I sit on the log in this woods of sighs and strange rustling. I get up and begin to push my way through gaps in the crowded branches and foliage. Brittle twigs poke at my jeans.

I imagine the visits the inmates of this relocation camp might have made into these same woods to try to get away from the crowds of people. Perhaps a teenage girl snuck out to be away from the tight, controlling old-country parenting. Because most of the first- and second-generation Japanese Americans would have been Shinto, I imagine many of them would come into this wooded part to pray. The *Kami* would have been here.

Shinto is the nature religion of the Japanese people. There is a mysterious power in nature. Shinto means "the way of the Kami." The Kami can be divine beings, the spirit of a particular place, such as a forest (in ancient

Greek terms, its *genius*), or the spirits of the dead. Some Kami are helpful; others can be harmful. One modern Shinto scholar has written,

> The Japanese people themselves do not have a clear idea regarding the Kami. They are aware of the Kami intuitively at the depth of their consciousness and communicate with the Kami directly without having formed the Kami idea conceptually or theologically. Therefore it is impossible to make explicit and clear that which fundamentally by its very nature is vague.[4]

How do we who are not of the Shinto tradition experience the Kami? I can become aware of them by seeing their effects in nature or by feeling for their presence. Certainly, inhabitants of this camp must have walked where I am walking now, communing with the Kami, praying for protection or, better, liberation and reunion with family back in Los Angeles.

I am walking toward the distinctive sound of crying. As I move into the center of the dark woods, I am disoriented. A huge old tree hovers over me and I cannot see the mountains in the west. I guess my direction by the sun and force myself painfully through the scratchy brush toward the source of the sound. And there it is: a piece of metal roofing from the old barracks lodged by some forgotten gale high up into this venerable cottonwood. The metal bends and scrapes against another tree and makes the sound of crying.

Suddenly a red blur races by my field of vision. When it has distance from me, it slows down. A bushy-tailed red fox. Certainly, a Japanese American walking and praying in these woods all those years ago would have instantly recognized that fox as the incarnation of a Kami, a messenger sent by the gods. But this particular Kami, the fox, is feared because it can possess people and cause illness and death. The fox darts a zigzag pattern under the barbed wire that protects the Manzanar cemetery to the west.

Then I notice a large white obelisk rising in the distance as the key memorial marker of those who died during the internment years. This monument was made in 1943 by one of the inmates, stonemason Ryozo Kado. The Japanese glyphs on the front face read: *Soul-Consoling Tower.* On the back of the monument is inscribed, *Erected by the Manzanar Japanese. August 1943.* As I draw close to the cemetery to look at the tower, I can see that it is decorated with strings of origami. Small memorials of stone have been left alongside children's toys and ceramic sake cups. There is a small cemetery with scattered graves, river rock outlining some of them. A

4. Ono, *Shinto*, 8.

few have concrete markers with the names of the deceased. I see a child's sunglasses on a headstone, which must mark the grave of a child. Another grave is decorated with a heart shaped out of barbed wire, perhaps taken from a fence around the camp. Here the dead are remembered and loved.

These beloved ancestor spirits are also a form of Kami. The inmates of the camp were removed from their own homes, where family altars maintained an ongoing connection with the dead. A photograph or some personal emblem of the deceased would be placed on that altar. There would be burning incense and food offerings, because those spirits must be remembered lest they become Obake, hungry ghosts. Obake are the restless spirits of people who have suffered injustice in this life—such as being removed from home and work and compelled to live behind barbed wire in a desolate desert.

Every year, on the last weekend of April, there is a pilgrimage to Manzanar when former inmates of the camp and their families journey here, many from Southern California. Certainly some of my Pasadena High School alums are among these pilgrims. The Manzanar Committee, which organizes this pilgrimage, refers to Manzanar as a concentration camp. It may be upsetting to read this, but that designation ties directly into the implication of President Franklin Roosevelt's Executive Order 9066 and the subsequent Public Law 503, which divided the USA into military districts that could be prohibited to any individual. The War Relocation Authority interpreted the order by prohibiting people of Japanese descent from much of the West Coast and interning them in ten relocation camps.

> Actually, there is substantial historical evidence of use of the term for the War Relocation Camps during World War II. President Roosevelt called them "concentration camps" in 1944, and the U.S. Attorney General referred to them as "concentration camps" in 1942. A wide range of politicians calling for the establishment of such camps in 1942 called them "concentration camps."[5]

Over the years, the events surrounding the pilgrimage have become more elaborate. Usually the UCLA Taiko Drummers perform a powerful cadence of ancient prayers. Films, lectures, and testimonies of former inmates fill the weekend of remembrance. Because this annual pilgrimage and remembrance of the difficult life in this camp highlight their common struggle for civil rights, recently the local Paiute tribal members and

5. Gordon Chappel, quoted in Forstenzer, "Bitter Feelings."

representatives of the Muslim community have participated in solidarity. Bruce Embrey wrote in the local newspaper, *The Inyo Register*:

> The similarities are uncanny between the kind of prejudice and racial profiling the Muslim and Arab Americans are facing now and the kind Japanese Americans endured in the 1940s.[6]

Cemetery Memorial at Manzanar, 2013. Author's collection.

6. Bruce Embrey, quoted in Bodine, "Pilgrimage to Honor Civil Rights Pioneers."

The April pilgrimage has become a vibrant gathering of Owens Valley Paiutes, the Muslim community, and families of the former Japanese inmates. A concluding event of this emotional weekend is a memorial service at the Manzanar cemetery. Christian, Jewish, Buddhist, and Muslim religious leaders participate. Most moving are the Shinto rituals for the dead, which are performed by a Shinto priest. During the years of World War II, the Shinto rituals had been forbidden by the camp director.

The best time to visit the Manzanar National Historic Site is between October and May, before the heat of summer. After you go to the visitor's center, you can secure a guide for driving the route around the camp. You will see a guard tower and several restored barracks. Archaeologists have resurrected ruins of the main buildings and the intricate network of waterworks and gardens that brought some serenity to the lives of the inmates. When you visit the cemetery, remember those who died, and let us all remember what happened here, so that it never happens again.

13

Kuichiro's Garden

You could face away from the barracks, look past a tiny rapids towards the
darkening mountains, and for a while not be a prisoner at all. You could stand
suspended in some odd, almost lovely land you could not escape from yet almost
didn't want to leave.

—JEANNE WAKATSUKI[1]

THE DREAM ENTERS MY sleep as a vivid visit to my childhood home on
Sierra Grande, set in two blocks of clustered homes inhabited by World
War II veterans and their families. In my dream I see the neighborhood
wedged between the mainline of the Santa Fe Railroad and Foothill
Boulevard (Route 66) in East Pasadena, California. Writing about it, I feel
a visceral longing for that long-ago place of sweet memories, where neigh-
bors were more like aunts and uncles than just "the people down the street."
The Technicolor dreams are clear and real. I hate it when they end.

When I make my regular visit to care for my aunt and uncle in Altadena, I drive west on the 210 Freeway towards downtown Pasadena, and
exit at Michillinda Avenue. The off-ramp passes directly over the neighborhood of my childhood, which is now buried under twenty feet of fill and
concrete, never to be seen again. There are other memories of other homes,
buried in sand and debris, that can be restored to light.

Kuichiro Nishi and his family had to leave their home in Los Angeles,
and their landscaping and nursery business, and were sent to Manzanar in
1942. Life was stressful there; the family lived in dormitories cheek by jowl
with ten thousand other displaced Japanese Americans, subject to blasting

---

1. Wakatsuki and Houston, *Farewell to Manzanar*, 99.

hot, dusty summers and stark, frigid winters. But Kuichiro Nishi would soon transform the bleak camp with a garden in Block 22.

Fortunately, camp director Ralph Merritt recognized Nishi's talent for bringing order and beauty to desolation and provided him with materials for constructing the remarkable Pleasure Garden, which was later to be named Merritt Park. It was a breathtaking design of waterfalls, ponds, a wooden bridge, a stone bridge, a tea room, a gazebo, lush plants, and above all, significant stones. It was a place of serenity and a gateway to the Holy for the people who had to live in Manzanar. The great photographer Ansel Adams made a famous picture of the place, and at the Manzanar Visitor Center you can view home movies of the garden as it once was in all its glory.

With the end of World War II, residents of the camp returned to their homes and the camp buildings were dismantled or sold off. The desert reclaimed the land with blowing sand and the occasional flash flood rushing out of the Sierra Nevada. When I drove through the camp twenty-five years ago, desert debris had buried Nishi's intricate and elaborate work. But in recent years the dedication of the Manzanar National Historic Site has breathed new life into the ruins of the camp, resurrecting buildings and, most importantly, the stories, so that what happened there would not be forgotten. Specialist archaeologists worked with volunteers to excavate Merritt Park. Among the volunteers were members of the Nishi family: Henry, Edith, and Barbara, three of Kuichiro's children. They joined others to carefully excavate brush, sand, and detritus from the park and to bring back to life their father's vision. Having participated in many archaeological excavations myself, I can imagine the family members on their knees, brushes in hand, carefully removing the desert's shroud. As they labored, handling the rocks and stooping close to the ground, memories sparked to life. They found voice to share stories about their father and what it was like for the family to live in this camp.

**Pool in Pleasure Park, Manzanar Relocation Center (Ansel Adams image).
County of Inyo, Eastern California Museum.**

During another desert retreat to the Owens Valley, in 2013, I discovered that J.R. and Marie Carillo Arnold, a couple who had worked as rangers and archaeologists in the reconstruction of Manzanar, were still living in Independence, a few miles to the north. I had blessed their marriage several years prior. They invited me to meet them at Merritt Park.

Again, a severe drought seems to be pressing hard on California. The Sierra Nevada has had only a dusting of snow and no rain in sight. But the pleasant fruit of the drought is a bright, sunny January day, 70 °F. These days always take my breath away. I park near the northwest corner of the camp and very soon I am immersed in an art and spirituality of which I had only a vague notion before. J.R. and Marie unfold for me an incredible tour of the Merritt Park. J.R. is a brilliant, inspired narrator, and he holds in his hand Sakuteiki's *Visions of the Japanese Garden.* This is the bible of the subject; written a thousand years ago, it is perhaps the oldest book on any kind of garden. I can see from the tattered pages of his copy that J.R. has embraced its learning and that becomes clearer as he leads me. Sakuteiki took his inspiration from the Chinese gardens of the Song Dynasty (960–1279 CE). J.R. points out how every boulder and rock in the garden is placed with great care to convey spiritual meaning. While Chinese gardens emphasized individual rocks resembling animals, Japanese gardens tended to emphasize the harmony of the whole layout. Sakuteiki provides specific yet strangely enigmatic direction for the arrangement of the rocks:

> Make sure that all the stones, right down to the front of the arrangement, are placed with their best sides showing. If a stone has an ugly-looking top, you should place it so as to give prominence to its side. Even if this means it has to lean at a considerable angle, no one will notice. There should always be more horizontal than vertical stones. If there are 'running away' stones there must be "chasing" stones. If there are "leaning" stones, there must be "supporting" stones.[2]

I have found that often I need a guide to help me appreciate the nuances of art. I can grasp colors, patterns, and textures, but I need someone who knows how to help me *see* what I am looking at, to integrate what it all means. The creative genius of Kuichiro Nishi was grounded in his own understanding of Sakuteiki. J.R.'s rapid-fire tour opened my eyes to the spiritual potency of the garden park.

Most Japanese garden ponds were either part of *tsukiyama* (hill gardens) or *hiraniwa* (flat gardens). J.R. points to the lower waterfall pond, which is in the shape of a tortoise, symbolic of longevity. I see a medium-size rock in the pond, also shaped like a tortoise. During the 1600s through the 1800s (the Momoyama to Endo Periods), tsukiyama was the most common garden design. Three important features were a waterfall, a stream, and a pond. Now I see a mound of earth crowned with a cluster of boulders. Water flows from this northern point, over the waterfall, which is fed by a natural stream, and moves south through the pond. J.R. says this pond could well have been home to local trout. I walk with J.R. and Marie to two large entry stones or steles with Japanese inscriptions. A recent pour of concrete outlines the site of the tea pavilion. A delicate stone bridge brings us to an island in the middle of the pond, which symbolizes the abode of the Taoist Heavenly Immortals.

2. Quoted from Marutschke, "Karesansui."

Merritt Garden in Restoration, 2014. Author's collection.

I am walking through a spiritual sanctuary that sustained and nurtured the people who had to live in this camp during World War II. While the Japanese nature religion of Shinto was severely repressed in Manzanar because of some aspects that honored the Japanese emperor, the stones surrounding me in this garden still have great spiritual power. They were a spiritual medium to induce the gods to bring blessings of health and good harvest. Through the influence of Buddhism, the precise placement of stones could be used for geophysical divination. Because they are seen as powerful and animate objects, the placement of these stones is at the heart of Japanese gardening. Sitting on a rock, meditating with the sound of running water and the expansive view of the Sierra Nevada in the distance, residents of the camp would have experienced intuitive connection to the Kami spirits.

We contemplate the garden in long silence. For a few moments, the dormant, leafless trees become lush and green, water gushes from the two waterfalls, and Japanese-American families cluster around the edges of the pond, children dipping and wiggling their little toes in the cool, flowing water. Surely God is in this place, Kuichiro's garden.

14

Contemplative Cows

What the Power of the Slowing taught me is what the Source of All constantly yearns for: that each one of us will know without doubt that we are loved, and that we are intimately, irrevocably part of the endless creation of love, and that we will join, with full freedom and consciousness, the joyous creativity that is Nature, that is Wildness, that is Wilderness, that is Everything.

—GERALD MAY, MD[1]

A LATE FEBRUARY STORM blew through the Owens Valley last night. As I drive on a rutted country road west of Highway 395 in Lone Pine, hazy morning clouds open up to radiant sunlight. This year, thankfully, the Sierra behind me to the west and the Inyo Mountains up ahead are covered with heavy snow almost to the valley floor. I pass a pioneer cemetery filled with sagebrush and willow. The narrow road abruptly makes a sharp right turn and I slow down in time to get a good look at an old horse trailer parked at a pasture entrance. There is a cowboy wearing a beaten old Stetson, long braided hair flowing down to the middle of his back. Can't see his face. He is leading a saddled brown quarter horse out of the trailer. As I pass him, I can read a sign painted on the side of the rig: "All-Indian Rodeo, Fallon, Nevada. Champion 1998." I recall that I am driving through the Lone Pine Paiute Indian Reservation and here is an Indian cowboy going to work.

The street is lined with huge old cottonwoods. This time of year the branches are barren, the bark is brittle, and they all look dead. In a month a green patina of buds will cover the tree as a sign that spring is coming.

---

1. May, *Wisdom of the Wilderness*, 190.

Free-range cattle, Owen's Valley, 2008. Author's Collection.

I am searching for a way to get down to the Owens River, which for the past eighty years has been a sad sump of debris and dying trees. But recently, the Los Angeles Department of Water and Power released water from the California Aqueduct into the river, and the valley's flora and fauna have begun to revive. I have not had a lot of luck getting close to this winding, meandering waterway, so today I have brought along a topographic map that shows a likely trail up ahead, branching off this road. I find the break in the barbed wire fence, park my Honda Pilot in the grass, button up my heavy jacket, and cross over to the other side of the road. I walk over a broad cattle guard, ribbed with steel bars to keep range cattle from wandering onto the highway. I see a winding line of cottonwoods in the distance, a hint that the Owens River must be there. The cow path drops lower into dense sand. A thousand years ago, the river was flowing right where I walk. I follow the cow path to a thicket of willow and birch trees. To my left I see a Black Angus cow standing beside a little black clump of something steaming; it is a calf born only in the last couple of hours. This is the time of year where newborn calves dot the rangeland of the Owens Valley. The mother bawls at me and I take notice, walking away quickly, not wanting to scare her. But she keeps up her alarm call. I walk towards the river, a rocky hill to my right. I hear another bellow from over there. Another cow is coming towards me at a fast trot with her baby keeping up beside her. And there is another cow following. Within minutes, I see twenty, fifty, a hundred more cows coming at me. It is a slow-motion stampede. I gingerly step back onto higher ground.

This is weird. Usually when I hike through the rangeland of the valley and come across a mother with her calf, they quickly run off. But all of these cows are moving closer and closer towards me. They are all mooing loudly, as if demanding some action on my part. At that very moment, the Indian cowboy appears, riding out of the sagebrush. He waves and smiles and rides down into the herd, paying careful attention to the calves. Then it hits me: dressed as I am in a heavy jacket and hightop Stetson, they think that I am the rancher, bringing hay to supplement their grazing. They are hoping for breakfast!

As you and I take our contemplative hikes through the dramatic landscape of the Owens Valley, we will see far more cattle than humans. I heard somewhere that there can be 25,000 head in the valley at one time. Cattle were brought here in the 1860s to feed the bustling mining camps of Bodie and Cerro Gordo. But, as often with species translation, problems followed. The cows ate the forage of the deer and elk, thus supplanting the native food sources of the Paiute people. As European Americans took over possession of this land, some Paiute adapted to the new conditions by becoming cowboys themselves. As such, a certain few became renowned.

Ranching is a hard life. Late winter and early spring is when calves are born, and that is when you will sometimes see cowboys riding the range to check on these precious bundles of new life. Brenda Lacey and her husband, Mark, have a cattle ranch near Independence. This post from her blog describes the difficult, dedicated work of raising cattle:

> Ever since the first of the year our main activity has been taking care of the first calf heifers. That is our term for a young cow that has never had a calf. They require extra feed, care and observation. These are first calf heifers. We keep them in a pasture of about 200 acres. When they start calving, approximately January 15th, we start riding through them horseback about three to four times a day. They are very inexperienced and do some dumb things. Some examples of heifer behavior are: giving birth just fine and then walking away —so we must find the heifer and take her back and try to bond her to the calf, some try to steal other heifer's calves, some can't give birth and we must assist the birth, occasionally

we have caesarian sections, sometimes the calves are weak and we must bottle feed them until they gain strength, some heifers won't accept their calves and we will graft them on to another heifer that is more maternal. When the calves are born they get an ear tag with their mother's number on it and source identification number that can be traced back to our ranch.

The calving season for the heifer is about 45 days. We start at about 4:00 a.m. and stay with the heifers until dark then we will make checks during the night if there are heifers that might calve.[2]

After a long, contemplative hike on the open rangeland, all the while being sensitive to my cattle companions, I nestle into a warm bed in my room at the famous Dow Villa Motel in Lone Pine. The cold night wind howls. Signage on Highway 395 sways precariously. Lights flicker. I think about those mother cows and their babies in the darkness. There are mountain lions and coyote packs out there. How do the cattle survive? All their senses must be in a state of heightened alertness to everything happening in the present moment.

John Lubken and Cattle at Lubken Ranch, Alabama Hills. County of Inyo, Eastern California Museum.

My mind shifts gears, as I stare into the dark ceiling of my room inviting the Lord's presence. Contemplation, like my praying in this present

2. Lacey, "Calving Season."

moment, must be some kind of awareness that is wide open and completely present to what is happening right now. But most of the time I am not so essentially aware. My culture and schooling have trained my brain to focus instead on specific tasks (such as typing these words) for which I must filter out background noises and maintain concentration. When we have long periods of focusing on a particular task, we become fatigued. You know the feeling. And even when we are not working on some specific task, our brains have been trained to tune out background stimuli.

Psychiatrist Gerald G. May has written a wonderful book called *The Wisdom of Wilderness: Experiencing the Healing Power of Nature*. He writes about contemplation in nature:

> It has always seemed to me that true natural presence, true wild being, involves no tuning out of anything. It must be absolutely contemplative—openly receptive to all the sights, sounds, smells, tastes, and feelings that exist in each immediate moment. I believe it is civilization, the taming of our nature, which has taught us to focus on a single task and tune out what we consider to be distractions. I acknowledge that we do not have to do this to function well in our society—but it just isn't natural.[3]

I am thinking of those baby calves in the open range of the Owens Valley. They are natural contemplatives. Mother cows teach their young ones not to focus on any one thing. They must keep their senses open and alert. The mother cow teaches her baby to "watch out for themselves, to remain open, and sensitive to sights, sounds and smells coming from any direction at any time."[4] Just as with the contemplative cows, our disabled son Erik has been my tutor in the contemplative potential of the present moment. I am too busy with my to-do list, focusing hard on this and that task. Doing just one thing at a time, I miss everything else. When I go for a walk with Erik after dinner on a summer evening, he is taking everything in. He is mentally three years old with the body of a twenty-nine-year-old man. I hold his hand as we walk, as his gait is unsteady. We walk to my commentary: "The leaves are rustling in the wind . . . the bird is singing . . . the yellow butterfly is flying . . . the sun is warm on our faces . . . the puffy clouds are floating in the blue sky." All is in the present moment. That is where Erik lives: little memory of the recent past, no fear or anxiety about the future. In our circle of love and care, Erik is fully present in this moment. He *is*.

3. May, *Wisdom of the Wilderness*, 61.
4. Ibid.

John and Artie Lubken, Chappo Bellas, Vin Hoagee, Fred Burkhardt, Cattle Branding Lone Pine. County of Inyo, Eastern California Museum.

Dr. May describes our difficulty in joining Erik and the cows in their gift of contemplation:

> Like domesticated animals, we are completely unprepared for the wild—the wild outdoors, the wild in our cities, the wild in our own psyches. In any of these places, we panic when we're lost and afraid. We frantically concentrate our attention here and there, following nonexistent tracks, unaware of a thousand clues from sky and light and smell and inner Wisdom that could tell us where to go and what to do. Feeling so divorced from the nature within and around us, we make wilderness an adversary that we must tame rather than join, master rather than learn from. Where we find it, we feel we must force Nature into the tunnel of our own concentrated vision.[5]

There is a gift in this spirit-soaked land. I have experienced it. Just as Kuichiro's garden is a surprise—the gifts of beauty and serenity rising from grim adversity—so you will surprise yourself. You come to the desert for your three or four days of contemplative walks. The first day you are concentrating on tasks unfinished, or focusing too much on this or that detail. But after a full day of walking through the landscape, the land and

5. Ibid., 65.

the presence of the Holy will make their claim on you. Mental and sensory filters will open up. Life will slow down and Grace will guide you by the hand into the present and you will be at home in yourself again.

15

Zane Grey and the Western Mystique

Surely, of all the gifts that have come to me from contact with the West, this one of sheer love of wilderness beauty, color, grandeur has been the greatest, the most significant for my work.

—Zane Grey[1]

As the moan of the cool wind, in the silken seep of sifting sand, in the distant rumble of a slipping ledge, in the faint rush of a shooting star he heard the phantoms of peace coming with whispers of the long pain of men at the last made endurable. . . . In the dead silence of the midnight hours he heard them breathing nearer on the desert wind—nature's voices of motherhood, whispers of God, peace in the solitude.

—Zane Grey[2]

A BRIGHT YELLOW STREAK on the triangular head of the Western diamondback rattlesnake glistened in the sunlight as my father held out his hand. The snake's mouth opened wide; huge yellow needle-sharp fangs, wet with saliva, emerged fully from their sheath of skin. My father was twelve then. He had been designated to help this marvelous snake-handling cowboy who went by the name of Zane Grey. The boy's hand trembled as the sound of the rattles grew louder and louder. Zane Grey said evenly and without alarm, "Hold steady, young man. Hold the stick steady in your hand."

1. Grey, "Man Who Influenced Me Most, " 136.
2. Grey, *Desert Gold*, 13.

Grey's grizzled assistant held the neck and the midsection of the seven-foot reptile. My father was clutching his two feet of balsawood. A circle of intent seventh-graders from Washington Junior High School was gathered around him and Zane Grey and the snake. No one was breathing; there was only the sound of the rattles. The assistant guided the snake's mouth to the stick and suddenly its fangs struck and lodged safely in the wood. The handler carefully moved the head back and forth and sideways as he milked the deadly poison into a glass jar, which Zane Grey held below the snake's head.

Everything safe, the cowboy addressed the group:

"Thank you Lyle. You have steady hands. All of you young people here know what this is? This is a Western diamondback rattlesnake, *Crotalus atrox*. You have probably seen this snake slithering in your own backyards, because most of you live up close to these mountains of Altadena. But don't bother these guys. They help your moms and dads by eating mice and rats and gophers. They won't bother you unless you bother them. So if you see one on the trail up to Echo Mountain, what do you do?"

One girl spoke: "Walk around it and keep your distance."

"That's right, young lady. Stomp those feet and let him know you are around and he will head off into the brush!"

This was just one of many encounters my father was to have with Zane Grey. Later on, at John Muir Technical High School, Grey's son, Loren, would become a close friend and mentor of my dad. Loren was a couple of years older than him and a terrific amateur photographer. He worked with my dad on the student newspaper and yearbook. My father remembers making many visits to the Grey's home at the foot of Echo Mountain in Altadena. He recalls the backyard with its menagerie of local animals such as that rattlesnake and the trophy heads of wild boar, mountain lion, and grizzly bear hanging from the adobe walls of the home of the famous writer.

I grew up in a house in which the bathroom cupboards were stuffed with tattered copies of Zane Grey novels. For most of his career, my dad traveled throughout Latin America as a contractor and field engineer, working on projects that involved concrete pumps. I would watch him methodically packing his suitcase; there was always a copy of a Zane Grey Western. I could picture my dad on long flights to Colorado or Mexico or Venezuela, devouring the stories again and again. Where did they take him in his imagination? Certainly the world that Zane Grey created seemed to give my father a sense of serenity and peace. Was it this that captured my father's loyal devotion to the novelist?

Serenity and a measure of contentment must have been at a premium in the life of my hard-working father. I remember his harrowing story about taking off in a plane during a thunderstorm from the airport in the then remote and exotic Quito, Ecuador. At the end of the runway was an abyss with a drop of thousands of feet that the pilot had to negotiate in his rickety, fuel-laden DC-3. Today, at ninety-five, Dad is full of details of these adventures, but mostly he talks about the loneliness and missing the family. As he read *Wanderer of the Wasteland* or *Desert Gold*, following the solitary travels of the protagonist, who might be clambering over endless desert sand dunes while evading a posse out for his skin, surely Dad's own long journeys along desert mountain passes and through dense jungles connected him with these stories. Perhaps he got the feeling that he was not alone in his loneliness, that someone had travelled this dangerous road before. I am thinking that, for my father, who was not an overtly religious person, reading the stories of his friend Zane Grey was his spirituality. The novels soothed the fires that burned within him. He found literary figures with whom he could deeply identify.

As you are traveling north on Highway 395 through Lone Pine, turn left at Whitney Portal Road, which ends at Whitney Portal, the base camp for climbing Mount Whitney. Horses graze in pastures as the road winds and climbs through a notch in the Alabama Hills. Gnarled, weirdly shaped boulders loom above us on both sides of the road. Here it helps if you are a movie buff. If you are, the first place you will recognize is the location of a scene in the Western monster film *Tremors*. The road levels out and the landscape expands to a vista of a 180 degrees. Turn right at Movie Road, drive a hundred yards or so, pull over, get out of your car and look! There is that iconic view of the Sierra Nevada and Mount Whitney. Robert Downey Jr., playing Tony Stark, stood right here as the hero of the movie *Iron Man*, demonstrating the power of his exploding weapons.

You are standing on the grand natural set of not only the Westerns made from Zane Grey's novels but also of many recent action films such as *Gladiator*, *The Lone Ranger*, *Man of Steel*, *Django Unchained*, and *Star Trek*. And over there Roy Rogers chased cattle rustlers. And Gene Autry crooned a cowboy ballad sitting in Champion's saddle amid that grouping of rocks.

From that bouldered canyon even the British India Army marched forth to the skirl of bagpipes in *Gunga Din.*

Zane Grey mounting up, ca. 1910. Lone Pine Film History Museum.

You can visit the Lone Pine Film History Museum at the south end of town to see exhibits about all the films created in this fertile womb of

Hollywood's imagination. The museum now has guidebooks with detailed directions inviting you to become a film detective in search of the locations of famous movies.

Walk with me towards that cluster of boulders. A cold wind is blowing, but in the shelter of the rocks the air becomes still and quiet. Usually I am alone when I come out here. As I consider the romance of the film stars who rode here—John Wayne, Gary Cooper, Clark Gable, Randolph Scott, Gregory Peck, and on and on—I sense the solitude of the Western heroes they portrayed. Stephen L. Tanner wrote an article about two novelists of the Wild West, Owen Wister and Zane Grey. He shows how they had experienced the West firsthand in the opening of the twentieth century:

> What they shared was the recognition that the West—its landscapes, people and cultures—was a very interesting place which presented a salutary contrast to the dehumanizing materialism and urbanization of the Gilded Age.[3]

For Zane Grey, encountering raw nature in the West was renewing and revitalizing. It purged the soul from sin and sorrow. Grey's spirituality of the West did not come from orthodox Christianity. It was shaped by the romantics of the previous century such as Rousseau, Emerson, and Thoreau. The heroes of Zane Grey's novels would retreat into the desert, often pursued by others or running away from personal tragedy. Spiritual revelation happens when blasting desert heat and deprivation in the wilderness strip away the glossy sheen of civilization. The filters that inhibit intuitive communion with nature fall away, and the hero finds redemption and salvation. The Western is a unique genre of literature evoking the vast landscape of the West and how it changes a person inside. Tanner recounts Zane Grey's first journey to Arizona and how it sparked his imagination. On that occasion he met a Mormon named Jim Emmet who taught him how to be present to nature in quiet, attentive observation, opening Grey's heart to the enchantment of the landscape. This so affected Grey that he could not but write of it for the rest of his life. There would be nearly sixty novels.

Wanderer of the Wasteland (1923) and *Shepherd of Guadalupe* (1930) are two of Zane Grey's tales that tell of solitary men who travel west to become healed or to find redemption after an act of violence. In the latter, Forrest takes up the work of a shepherd, which involves marked solitude. Forrest is convinced that God has abandoned him, but as his heart opens

---

3. Tanner, "Spiritual Values in the Popular Western Novel."

in intuitive communion with nature, he receives new eyes to perceive the wonders and enchantments around him. These are the makings of a desert mystic. His solitary life in the desert soothed the painful memories of the past and awakened "a spiritual consciousness stronger than anything in primal nature. While there was life there was hope, good, truth, joy and God."[4] As Zane Grey writes about the West, the spiritual power of nature and landscape are the healing and redemptive resources of the Holy.

The Braniff Airlines plane from Mexico City to Quito, Ecuador, tries to fly over a storm, but the clouds are too massive. While the plane tosses and shakes, my father is buried in another tattered Zane Grey novel. Reading Grey's stories calmed him amidst the literal and metaphorical storms of life. While his business trips to exotic locations could be exciting and surprising, how he missed our family! The long separation and the solitude wore on his soul. As he read about the wandering desert heroes, did he find the context in which he could work with his own burden of solitude?

The Western Channel on our cable television network now brings me twenty-four-hour access to Western films and the stories of Zane Grey. Our new HDTV presents vivid images of John Ford's landscapes of the desert and the famous sandstone formations of Monument Valley in Utah. Like no other genre of film, the Western resonates with a visceral longing for something. What is it? Do you ever have that feeling?

Our increasingly busy lives, our instant connectivity, our fancy electronics, all wear down our attention. Stress comes at us from all sides. Even in retirement (as I have found), tension continues. We all long for a peaceful place apart, of solitude and quiet, where we can rest.

I can calendar another desert retreat to the Owens Valley or the Mojave Desert where I can commune again with the Holy Presence. I can do all the preparations, pack all the necessities, and plan for a good retreat. But that does not necessarily mean that in the desert retreat I will make a connection with the Holy. In his article "Longing for Solitude," Ron Rolheiser writes, "Solitude cannot be so easily programmed. It has to find us, or, more accurately, a certain something inside us has to be awakened to its presence." When I go on a desert retreat in the Owens Valley I plan for at least three days. The first day or two, walking alone on crunching desert

4. Grey, *Shepherd of Guadaloupe*, 204.

sands, I will be alone. The busy mind will continue to spin out memories, conflicts, and work left undone. So much chatter going on! Then the continued physical exertion of long walks, climbing up mountain trails, slows my mind so that I can become more attentive to the present moment, what is happening right in front of me. Often by the third day, the kindness of solitude seeps in and my senses awaken to the deeper tastes, smells, and sounds of the natural world around me. This is the gateway to wonder and the embrace of the Holy.

16

Searching for the Hidden Ashram

The longest journey is the journey inward.

—DAG HAMMARSKJÖLD[1]

The fourth condition is Atman in his own pure state: the awakened life of supreme consciousness. It is neither outer nor inner consciousness, neither semi-consciousness nor unconsciousness. He is Atman, the Spirit himself, that cannot be seen or touched, that is above all distinction, beyond thought and ineffable. In the union with him is the supreme proof of his reality. He is the end of evolution and non-duality. He is peace and love.

—MANDUKYA UPANISHAD[2]

MY GOOD FRIEND SISTER Eileen McNerney, CSJ, asked me recently whether I had a spiritual bucket list. We were at lunch, but I don't think it was a casual enquiry. The phrase comes from the 2007 movie *The Bucket List*, in which two men of quite different backgrounds share a hospital room. Both have terminal cancer. They create a list of all the things they want to do before they "kick the bucket," and then they go out and do all they can of the list. In sharing many exhilarating experiences they become fast friends and find joy in each other and in the memories of their lives.

Sister Eileen set me thinking: what would appear on my bucket list? For one thing, I think I would like to go back to the town of Braunschweig

1. Hammarskjöld, *Markings*, 58.
2. Mascaro, trans., *Upanishads*, 85.

in Germany to visit the Heimbs family and Saint Andreas Church. I was there during two crises in my life: determining my vocation to the priesthood, and during struggles in my marriage. There are also many people who have been formative in my life whom I would like to see again. In fact, the list would consist mostly of people and places—those transformative places where encounters with the Holy have changed my life. No, this is not the sort of list that includes "peak experiences" where testosterone and adrenalin rule; I can leave the bungee jumping for another time. There is a deep longing in each of us for transformative communion with the Holy. For some of us our longing has yet to be fulfilled, but for others, if we have experienced the Holy in a particular place, then surely we are drawn there again. A pilgrimage is in our future. And the same applies if somehow we know the Holy is in a particular place that we have not yet visited.

High on my list is a visit to the ashram hidden in the Sierra foothills west of Lone Pine, California.

Ashram, Lone Pine, ca. 1980. County of Inyo, Eastern California Museum.

The front door to the Alabama Café jingles, announcing new arrivals for breakfast on this warm April day. It is the sort of intimate diner where everyone is more or less aware of everyone else's business. My window seat gives me a direct view of Mount Whitney, which is reflecting the golden aura of the sun rising over Death Valley. At the booth behind me there are two mountain guides comparing notes for an expedition that will begin today. A young man and woman come in, see the guides, wave in recognition and join them. I listen in as introductions are made. Soon the booth has eight occupants. They get down to business: the guides carefully check off who brought what for the ascent of Mount Langley, a peak not as heavily trodden as Mount Whitney and which therefore entails greater precautions.

An elderly rancher and two of his hands enter, spurs ringing. They sit at the table across from me shouting greetings to the waitress and friends at the counter. Their talk is about repairing fences and the cow that struggled last night to give birth, needing a cowboy's help with a chain around the calf's legs and a strong, steady pull. All turned out well with mother and baby.

During a lull, I get the attention of the waitress and ask her, "Do you know anything about the ashram up in the hills?" A hush descends on the room as though I had asked something indelicate. Had I broken a taboo?

"Why do you ask?" she replies.

"I heard about it from my friend, Chris Langley. Do you know how to get there?"

"Haven't been there myself," she confessed, "but I understand that if you go up Whitney Portal Road and turn left at . . ." A thirty-something man at the counter interrupts her.

"Don't be giving that information away, Lucy. We do like to keep that location a secret." A beat, and the routine banter resumes in the café as though I had not asked the question. And I certainly was not going to repeat it.

I have consulted maps and hiking reports and this is what I have come up with: from Lone Pine, turn west onto Whitney Portal Road, then turn south onto Horseshoe Meadows Road, then west on Granite View Drive and follow the road to the parking area at the end. Follow the Tuttle Creek Trail to the ashram. Chris Langley says it is about a two-hour hike, but after my three surgeries I hesitate to venture forth alone, and today I am on my own. Of all the sacred sites I have written about, the ashram must remain, for the time being at least, on my spiritual bucket list.

What exactly is an ashram, after all? It is no more or less than a hermitage, a place for spiritual retreat. There are countless such places in India, set apart in forest or mountain, where today people go to receive spiritual instruction from a guru, a teacher, and to practice yoga and meditation. India gave birth to the ashram during a period of dramatic spiritual transformation. During the Late Vedic Era (or Brahmanic Age, ca. 800–400 BCE), the spiritual practices of India became extremely complicated. Elaborate sacrifices involving many priests over a period of as much as a year cut off the common people from participation.

I imagine this to have similarities with what happened in the United States during the late 1960s when we experienced a significant shift from traditional religious ways and theological assumptions. With the influence of the open door to Asian immigration and the concurrent influx of Zen, Buddhist, and Hindu spiritual practices, the religious landscape of the nation was transformed. There was a Great Awakening, which continues to this day, involving in many a deep hunger for personal, life-changing spiritual experience.

In response to the complexity of the Brahmanic cults that had developed during the Late Vedic Age in India, it became usual for people to travel to the forests and mountains to sit at the feet of one spiritual master or another who had established his ashram far from the crowded towns. All people, whatever their caste or sex, were able to do this. During this time, the insightful teachings of these masters about the nature of reality and their answers to the deepest human longings were colligated into what would become the 112 Upanishads.

The Upanishads remind me of the Christian New Testament. The Gospels are suffused with aphoristic sayings of Jesus such as, "I and the Father are one" (Jn 10:30). There is a similar spirit in the Upanishads. We have an innate desire for union with God. The Indian gurus revealed that God (Brahman) is the ultimate reality behind all things and that God is not separate from humans but is at the inmost part of us (Atman).

I will summarize the essentials of this Indian worldview because it connects directly with the energy and inspiration that has built and sustained the Ashrama near Lone Pine. These are elements that differ from the themes of the monotheistic Abrahamic religions, Judaism, Christianity, and Islam. Yes, the terminology can be daunting to some people, but the ideas held within are sublime and subtle, and the special words are important here.

Samsara: *that which flows together.* The world has a mysterious flexibility that includes many forms of reality that flow together. All energy and matter are conserved and are being constantly and dynamically transformed. All living things are continuously reborn. If this idea of reincarnation sounds way off base, see what David Toolan, SJ, a quantum physicist and Jesuit priest, has to say:

An organism is an information and thermodynamic system, receiving, storing and giving off both energy and information in all its forms, from the light of the sun to the flow of food, oxygen and heat passing through it.

Like the sun and moon, we are disturbances in the field, vortices in turbulent nature. We are probably the most recycled beings in the universe, even while we live, dissolving and re-enfleshing. We regrow our entire physical body as we do our hair and nails. Nothing in our genes was present a year ago. The tissue of our stomach renews itself weekly, the skin is shed monthly and the liver is regenerated every six weeks. At every moment a portion of the body's 10^{28} atoms is returning to the world outside and ninety percent of them are replaced annually. Each time we breathe we take in a quadrillion atoms breathed by the rest of humanity within the last two weeks and more than a million atoms breathed personally by each person on earth.[3]

Does that expand your understanding of reincarnation? The Romantic poet Rainer Maria Rilke adds this imagery:

Ah,

Not to be cut off

Not through the slightest partition

Shut out from the law of the stars.

The inner—what is it?

If not intensified sky, hurled through with birds and

Deep with winds of homecoming.[4]

Karma: *the spiritual law that determines our next birth.* We are not born with a clean slate, but we carry the heritage of our previous lives. All action has consequence. The bad karma that comes from harming any living thing can result in our return as a lizard in the next life. This provides an interesting answer to the problem of evil: it may seem as if people get away with doing wrong in this life, but the next time around things will be set right.

Duhkha: *dissatisfaction.* As much as I long to arrive at a state of happiness that may be found in personal achievement, possessions, and relationships, I will always be dissatisfied. This is not a matter for dark depression

---

3. Toolan, *At Home in the Cosmos*, 188.

4. From "Ah, Not to Be Cut Off," in Rilke, *Ahead of All Parting*, 191.

but the door that opens on enlightenment and liberation (*Moksha*), which is described below in the Crest Jewel.

Vivekachudamani, the Crest Jewel: *Brahman is the Only Truth.* The world is unreal, and there is ultimately no difference between Brahman and the individual self. To gain the Only Truth there are four things that I must recognize and embrace:

- A necessary identity crisis. The constant change and flux in the world torments me. No matter how much I wish for permanence, nothing stays the same. But I must acknowledge that all I possess, all that I love, will be taken from me one way or another.

- An appreciation of what I am *not*. I have spent a lifetime creating and defending a False Self. This illusion has me wrong-footed. But inevitably my False Self will be uncovered. For this to happen I need an ashram where there is a teacher who can lead me from the unreal to truth.

- I must find my True Self through an appropriate yoga.

- In celebrating the One True Self (Atman) that has always lived within me, my life will change forever.

Yoga: *to yoke or harness a discipline.* This is the way to achieve release from *Samsara* and the cycle of life, death, and rebirth. Right now you may be thinking of that yoga class you take at the health club to relieve stress or to become more flexible in body. But at an ashram the term refers to the various spiritual disciplines that help you use your own body and breath to quiet the rapid-fire mind so your True Self can be with God—Atman in communion with Brahman.

The world enchants and entangles our minds; it blazes out in some kind of frenetic fireworks display that seduces our consciousness into continuing its journey to nowhere. The way out of the whirl is for consciousness to embrace this high drama and to yoke it to spiritual practice.

Professor Huston Smith, who taught me world religions at UC Berkeley, considers that the genius of religion in India has to do with how it adapts to the makeup of the individual. He told us to consider that our unique selves have been dealt a hand at cards. Playing cards have four suits. Each of us has a dominant one in our hand: hearts, spades, clubs, or diamonds. I tell my own students to consider the Myers-Briggs personality test, which shows that each of us has some dominant characteristic. The genius of spirituality in India is that at least one of the different kinds of yoga is a suitable discipline for each personality in bringing a person into communion with God. Here are four kinds of yoga and the personality types they would match.

Janana Yoga. This is for the reflective person who takes the path of knowledge. With the help of a wise teacher you can develop intuitive insight into the depths of Scripture to the point that the ideas dance in the head. By this means we are guided to the Atman and self-realization.

> After negating all of the above-mentioned as "not this," "not this," that Awareness that alone remains—that I am. . . . The thought "who am I?" will destroy all other thoughts, and like the stick used for stirring the burning pyre, it will itself in the end get destroyed. Then there will arise Self-realization.[5]

Karma Yoga. This is for the action-oriented personality. It embraces all useful activity that is done with detachment, without desire or for reward. I think of the Christian notion of *agape* as being similar. Here is something Swami Vivekananda has to say in connection with the activity called work:

> But with this secret we must take into consideration the great objection against work, namely that it causes pain. All misery and pain come from attachment. I want to do work. I want to do good as a human being; and it is ninety-to-one that the human being whom I have helped will prove ungrateful and so go against me and the result to me is pain. Such things deter mankind, this fear of pain and misery.[6]

Bhakti Yoga. This is for the emotive personality. An example of this form of practice would be in the daily *puja* at the home altar, sharing a love relationship with a beloved deity such as Krishna or Shiva; anointing an image, singing to and offering food with devotion of one's whole heart.

Royal Yoga. This is for the contemplative personality. Yogis say that it is easier to calm a wild tiger than it is to quiet the mind, which is like a drunken monkey that has been bitten by a scorpion. But the mind is the gateway to the True Self. The goal of Royal Yoga is to make the mind absolutely calm and clear. It involves a course of eight graded steps, the Eight Limbs, which help to harness the breath and the body so that after much effort one can go to that deep, fourth level of consciousness, Atman, gaining

5. Maharishi, *Who Am I?*, #2, 10.
6. Vivekananda, *Complete Works*, vol. 2, 361.

Ultimate Reality, union with God. This super-conscious state of union with God, the goal of Royal Yoga, is called *Samadhi.*

Ashram, with view of Owens Valley, ca. 1980. County of Inyo, Eastern California Museum.

In 1928, the Harvard philosopher and mathematician Franklin Merrill-Wolff made a spiritual pilgrimage with his wife, Sherifa, to the Owens Valley, camping at the base of Mount Whitney for several weeks. The landscape captured their hearts and they decided to create a school there for spiritual exploration, open to all seekers. Influenced by Sufi, Buddhist, and Muslim mystics, Franklin had already experienced the first of several awakenings whereby he knew with great clarity—"I am Atman." The Sufi sage Hazrate Inayat Kahn directed Franklin and Sherifa to establish their school at what was then the highest mountain in the country, Mount Whitney. The serene, remote Tuttle Creek became the setting of their ashram.

In conversation with my friend Chris Langley, he reflected on his profound connection with this place and with his teacher, Franklin Wolff:

> I had been travelling the world as part of my Peace Corps assignment when I finally arrived in Lone Pine. It seemed ironic that after searching out there for a teacher, I would discover Dr. Merrell-Wolff at the base of Mount Langley, the mountain named after my great-great-grandfather. I studied with him for a good part of

the next ten years. Many years before, he and his students had built the Ashrama at the base of Langley as a karma yoga exercise by day, followed by *Satsang* sessions in the evenings.

I began a rather intensive program of study with Franklin and his students, every Sunday and Wednesday night. At that point the Ashrama had suffered abuse from the weather and, worse, the federal government. The area had been designated a wilderness and roofed buildings were not allowed. They intended to dynamite the Ashrama, but then realized that it would not be a good solution. Reducing the buildings to a pile of rocks would not remove it as a "blight" on the viewscape. The buildings also had cultural and historical significance. My studies were an extremely important part of my spiritual development and the Ashrama represented a physical manifestation of Dr. Wolff's introceptualism. It remains that today, although much of the structure has been stripped of the symbolic aspects of its architecture.

For myself, I have wondered what it was about Franklin Wolff's teaching that connected with Chris. As a philosophy professor who has taught for almost forty years, I have reviewed some of Wolff's lecture notes on the Internet and I find his teachings to be dense and very difficult to understand. My first thoughts are that this good man, through yoga and deep contemplative meditation, had profound noetic encounters with the Holy that words cannot capture. After all, that is the nature of mysticism: the intuitive communion with Ultimate Reality is ineffable.

I believe that Wolff must have embodied his mystical experiences in such a way that there was a kind of luminescent aura about him, a congruence of word and spirit that said to his students, " I have been there, I have seen the Real. I am so filled with this Spirit that I am compelled to help you in your journey to union with God." Fortunately, there is a film of a lecture by Dr. Wolff made towards the end of his life,[7] so that you can experience some of what I am talking about yourself.

In an article Chris Langley wrote for the *Territorial Review Monthly*, November 2008, he remembers the Ashrama:

> Nearly every year I find my way up there at least once. This year I made the hike with my son, daughter-in-law and three grandchildren. I was happy I was still healthy enough to make the trek. It is not a particularly hard walk, but it is all uphill!

7. Bray, "Interview with the Sage," online at https://www.youtube.com/watch?v=BIMazReCp28.

At first the Ashrama itself is difficult to make out, perched on the steep canyon walls as it is. It actually sits on a pinnacle of rock in a magnificent setting. I remember the students remarking on how the location had been chosen. Dr. Wolff and his wife Sherifa had wanted to be near the highest point in the lower forty-eight states. The students also said the place was the location of intersecting ley-lines, a power center for earth energy, acknowledged by both early Indian inhabitants and wild animal trails as well. . . . The two thousand square-foot building in the form of a balanced cross symbolizes the principle of equilibrium.[8]

Students of Wolff have come to call the building the Ashrama and continue to hold a conference there every year in August. Residents of Lone Pine (if they will speak to you at all on the subject) call it the Monastery. Hiking guidebooks refer to the site as Stone House.

What is on your spiritual bucket list? In India, the first and second stages of life are known as *student* and *householder*, respectively. The third stage, after the family has been raised—what those of means might call "retirement"—is the time to go off to a forest or mountain ashram to seek spiritual communion with the Holy.

In my experience as a parish priest, as we live through this spiritual Great Awakening in our culture, I encounter increasing numbers of middle-aged students, parishioners, and friends who pay attention to that inner call for communion with the Holy. Even though I have not yet made it to the Ashrama, I hope what I share here will encourage you to give your heart fully to the inward journey.

8. Langley, "Living in the Land of 20 Mile Shadows."

17

Temptation in the Desert

The lone and level sands stretch far away.
—Percy Bysshe Shelley[1]

Like a roaring lion your adversary the devil prowls around, looking for someone to devour
—1 Peter 5:8

THE HOT, DRY DESERT breeze flows through the open windows of Father Spellacy's quarters at the Santa Isabella Mission on the edge of the Mojave Desert. The priest pulls aside the torn grey curtains to contemplate the scene outside: a graveyard of moldering wooden headboards and a looming concrete angel that is missing an arm. The whole is in the shadow of an immense lightning-scarred cottonwood. Father Spellacy's Jesuit-style soutane is missing half its buttons and the black has faded to an indeterminate color. This is the establishing shot of the 1981 film *True Confessions*, a crime drama. The scene closes the movie too.

It is Los Angeles in the late 1940s. Father Desmond Spellacy (played by Robert De Niro) had been a rising star of the ecclesiastical firmament, a favorite of Cardinal Danaher. He was adept at bringing in church projects under budget, and he put this talent at the service of his career. He had gained the papal distinction of Monsignor, which is a step away from a bishopric. Yes, ethics had been compromised as he got church business

---

1. "Ozymandias," in Shelley, *Selected Poetry and Prose of Shelley*, 194.

done, but he had persuaded himself to focus on the big picture. The priest's brother, Tom (played by Robert Duvall), is a nose-to-the-ground detective with an old-fashioned respect for justice and a tenacious, naïve piety that, for Father Spellacy, has gone by the wayside.

A young woman has been murdered. As the investigation proceeds, the brothers' personal allegiances—one for advancement in Mother Church, the other for justice—collide. The priest must decide between siding with his brother against evil or with his own pursuit of power and glory. By the final scene, the priest has chosen to cooperate with his brother in bringing a key benefactor of the Church before the law. As a result, he is exiled to the desert outpost. His hair is grey and he is gravely ill with a diseased heart. He gazes out the window at the cemetery where soon he will be laid to rest. There is serenity in his face, and joy at having rejoined his beloved brother. The exile is not a punishment but a spiritual homecoming.

My first bishop, Robert C. Rusack, who ordained me priest in 1971, was the last of the prince-bishops of the Episcopal Church. He came from a middle-class New England family, married a wealthy heiress, and was chosen as suffragan bishop in the diocese of Los Angeles when still young. He was ambitious and had the drive to become bishop. He adopted a careful strategy of cultivating close ties with all the clergy, always writing thank you notes at the faintest opportunity. His efforts resulted in his being elected bishop of Los Angeles on the first ballot. He could also be a stern, difficult, and distant father figure to us clergy. He dearly loved the "smells and bells" of the Catholic liturgy and he was a wonderful teacher and pastor. I remember the day he surprised us in a sermon at a clergy retreat when he said that his favorite movie was *True Confessions*. He always wept when he watched it—not something a New Englander would readily avow. I am guessing that in the movie he saw reflected his own ambition and perhaps some compromises made in the course of time: things done and left undone. Maybe in his mind Bishop Robert stood by Robert De Niro gazing at the little cemetery and the vast desert beyond, clearly understanding the lesson of the cinematic drama: human projects and pursuits in themselves are futile; we die, and all our machinations add up to naught.

As it happened, beloved by the clergy and laity of his diocese and having made his work his life, Bishop Robert died of a heart attack during dinner at home.

For some the desert is a place of danger and deprivation; for others it is the place of purgation and penance where one wrestles with temptation and evil spirits, within and without. For me, the consistent visceral feeling has been that I am at home in the desert. It is where God touches my heart with grace and love. And that scene at the window of the priest's adobe has lived with me since I first saw Ulu Grosbard's movie.

Looking back on forty-three years as a priest, I had many ambitious dreams when I started out. I wanted to be a pastor in Beverly Hills, then bishop of Massachusetts. I went to a goal-setting workshop and wrote a personal five-year plan that called for my moving from the Logan barrio of Santa Ana to be pastor of some affluent parish with a large staff and collection baskets full of cash. In this way, I told myself, I could command more resources "to help people." Those five years turned into ten, but still I pushed myself towards upscale opulence, and actually almost made it happen. For one reason or another—a (fortunate) choice here or there, my son's ill-health, and so on—those ten years turned into thirty and I found myself still where God had put me. And I thank God for that every day.

Among the many blessings, those were thirty years of waking at three in the morning to worry about where I was going to find the money to keep open the early childhood center for very poor children, as it competed for funds and time and space and talent with twenty other essential and worthy ministries. I was the point man; it was up to me. Funding crises always seemed to happen during my vacation—some vacation! Images of the innocent children and the anxious mothers would play in my half-dreams. If only I could arrive at that secure place, that creative space where there were no desperate emergencies to allay, no flare-ups to smother. Urban ministry was a relentless battle. I was driving on vapors.

And where in my desperation did I always find God's daily grace, God's amazing grace, to get me through each seemingly intractable problem but in the desert? There it was, all I needed, and in abundance. Walking in the desert saved me from temptation, my temptation to build an empire of worldly success centered on myself. Just as the Hebrews had to learn to be dependent on God for their survival in the desert, I went to the desert to learn the same. I was walking with Jesus in the desert when I was saved.

Jesus leads us into the desert. Jesus, our spiritual pioneer. Christians believe that Jesus is the fully human and fully divine Son of the Living God, the God of the prophet Abraham. I imagine that Jesus slowly became aware of who he was. It was as though he struggled to overcome some sort of amnesia in making sense of his deep longing for his connection, his iden-tity, with Abba-Father-God. And it was his own time in the desert that sparked into full flame the awareness of his True Self.

> Jesus, full of the Holy Spirit, returned from the Jordan and was led by the Spirit in the wilderness, where for forty days he was tempted by the devil. He ate nothing at all during those days, and when they were over, he was famished. The devil said to him, "If you are the Son of God, command this stone to become a loaf of bread." Jesus answered him, "It is written, 'One does not live by bread alone.'" Then the devil took him up higher and showed him all the king-doms of the world in a single instant. He said to him, "I will give you all the power and the glory of these kingdoms. The power has been given to me and I give it to whomever I wish. Prostrate yourself in homage before me, and it shall be yours." In reply, Jesus said to him, "Scripture has it, 'You shall do homage to the Lord your God; him alone shall you adore.'" Then the devil led him to Jerusalem, set him on the parapet of the temple, and said to him, "If you are the Son of God, throw yourself down from here, for Scripture has it, 'He will bid his angels watch over you'; and again, 'With their hands they will support you, that you may never stumble on a stone.'" In reply, Jesus said to him, "It also says, 'You shall not put the Lord your God to the test.'" When the devil had finished all the tempting, he left him to await another opportunity. (Luke 4:1–13)

In a presentation on this passage, Father Henri Nouwen helped me see that Jesus was wrestling with his True Self in that desert. When he refused to turn stones into bread, Jesus did not choose the lie that says, "I am only what I do." Jesus did not jump off the parapet of the temple to choose the lie, "I am what people say about me." Jesus turned his back on honoring Satan and choosing possessions over his True Self. He would not say, "I am what I have." In the desert, Jesus encountered God's loving presence and his True Self as the Beloved One.

Perhaps you will meet the same temptations that I encounter every time I first walk alone in silence and solitude in my desert journeys. I have described before how the busy mind begins to quiet as I take in the stark, vast wildness. Usually the only sounds are the wind rustling through the sagebrush and creosote bushes and the sand crunching under my boots. Very soon a voice creeps up on me: memories bubble up from the distant past—perhaps of the people I have hurt in some way. It is like a slap in the face. I often will cry aloud, "I am so stupid! How could I have done such a thing to that person?" Even though I have been through this many times over the years and can anticipate the snare, that voice still speaks, grabs me, and slaps me about. It is very hard to escape its grasp. Temptation—that is its nature.

Henri Nouwen knew exactly what I am talking about. In a message entitled, "Being the Beloved," he describes exactly my temptation:

> Over the years I have come to realize that the greatest trap in life is not success, or popularity or power, but self-rejection. Success, popularity, and power can indeed present a great temptation, but their seductive quality often comes from the way they are part of the much larger temptation to self-rejection. When we have come to believe in the voices that call us worthless and unlovable, then success, popularity, and power are easily perceived as attractive solutions. The real trap, however, is self-rejection. As soon as someone accuses me or criticizes me, as soon as I am rejected, left alone, or abandoned, I find myself thinking, "Well, that proves once again that I am a nobody." My dark side says that I am no good. . . . I deserve to be pushed aside, forgotten, rejected, and abandoned. Self-rejection is the greatest enemy of the spiritual life because it contradicts the sacred voice that calls us "the Beloved." Being the Beloved constitutes the core truth of our existence.[2]

When that dark presence tries to possess me, I ask Jesus to walk close with me and eventually another part of my consciousness opens to other memories, memories of how grace and blessing have always come in desperate times: Erik in the hospital, struggles in our marriage, awaking to debilitating pain after six hours of surgery. Those memories of being at the end of my resources open into remembrance of how God has come to me again and again, of how hope, peace, joy, and love slowly seep into the cracks and empty spaces in my heart. The demons of painful memories and sin give way to angels of mercy and to my gratitude. Every time I go into the desert, expecting nothing, it has sparked into life memories for which I can be only deeply grateful, memories of how I too am God's Beloved.

This book has invited you to walk with me alongside the great sages of holy wisdom into the spiritual crucible of the desert. I do understand that there are other places where we encounter the Holy and the Truth, and that wherever we are, as my son Erik teaches me, we are home and God is there. But there is still something about this desert . . .

2. Nouwen, "Being the Beloved."

In my many encounters with residents of the Owens Valley, I have heard touching stories about how people came to live here. The vast desert landscape tugged at their hearts so strongly that they could not but leave their other lives behind them to come and dwell in this spiritually charged place. Recently, Roberta Harlan, Curator of Exhibitions at the Eastern California Museum in Independence, shared with me her story about her successful career as a librarian elsewhere. But there was something about the Owens Valley that lingered deep in her consciousness and eventually these longings brought her here. She is very happy that this happened.

After a long hike through canyons in the Rose Valley, north of Little Lake, I see a cave midway up a volcanic basalt face. Crumbling piles of debris lead up to the mouth of the cave. I enter the tight space, find a flat rock near the entrance, and sit to appreciate the wide vista below me. Silence. Silence— except for the gentle wind. I call to mind Saint Anthony of the desert.

He was one of the first Christian ascetics to go into the Egyptian desert wilderness, in about 270 CE. He was the scion of a wealthy family but he had heard the words of Jesus, "If you want to be perfect, go, and sell what you have, and give to the poor, and you will have treasure in heaven; and come, follow me" (Matt 19:21). Anthony gave the family land to his neighbors and retreated to the desert for communion with God. There he intentionally sought solitude in the harsh wilderness. His spiritual struggles became the stuff of legend: the dark voices within him showed themselves as wild beasts, snakes, and scorpions. In the mind of the nascent church, he was considered one of the first of the desert fathers, the "first master of the desert and the pinnacle of holy monks." The irony is that his manifest holiness drew others to him and he had to go deeper and deeper into the desert to escape them.

In a cave, perhaps like this one in which I contemplate him, Anthony tries to hide from the demons that pursue him, haunt him. Relentless assaults on his physical body, beatings, leave him close to death. Suddenly, a heavenly light flashes and chases the demons out of his cave. Anthony revives and recognizes that God has intervened. He calls out to God:

> "Where were you when the demons were trying to beat me to death?" And God answers, "I was here but I would abide to see thy battle, and because thou hast many fought and well maintained thy battle, I shall make thy name to be spread through all the world."[3]

---

3. "Life of Saint Antony," in Voragine, *Golden Legend*, vol. 2.

Ron Rolheiser has a good take on what the unique power of the desert is about:

> The desert, as we know, is the place where, stripped of all that normally nourishes and supports us, we are exposed to chaos, raw fear and demons of every kind. In the desert we are exposed, body and soul, made vulnerable to be overwhelmed by chaos and temptations of every kind. But, precisely because we are so stripped of everything we normally rely on, this is also a privileged moment for grace. Why? Because all the defense mechanisms, support systems and distractions that we normally surround ourselves with so as to keep chaos and fear at bay, work at the same time to keep much of God's grace at bay. What we use to buoy us upwards off both chaos and grace, demons and the divine alike. Conversely, when we are helpless we are open. That is why the desert is both the place of chaos and the place of God's closeness. It is no accident that Dorothy Day and Martin Luther King felt God's presence so unmistakably just at that point in their lives where they had lost everything that could support them. They were in the desert. Scripture assures us that it is there that God can send angels to minister to us.[4]

---

4. Rolheiser, "Desert – Place of God's Closeness."

18

A Reluctant Mystic

We are fired into life with a madness that comes from the gods. . . . It has us
believe that we can have a great love, that we can perpetuate our own seed and
that we can contemplate the divine.

—PLATO[1]

Long before we do anything explicitly religious at all, we have to do something
about the fire that burns within us. What we do with that fire, how we channel it,
is our spirituality.

—FR. RON ROLHEISER, OMI[2]

BURIED SOMEWHERE IN MY head was the story of a young woman of seventeen who had had a powerful encounter with some sort of Presence in the
desert. It was an unusual story, but not unique. Then I read recently something that brought the event front and center: the encounter had happened
in Lone Pine, California, the little town in the middle of my own spiritual
homeland, the Owens Valley.

Barbara Ehrenreich is now in middle age and a science writer. She
grew up in a staunchly atheistic family culture in which reason and ra-
tionality were the measures of truth. But during a camping trip in Lone
Pine in 1959, something happened to her that pierced this secure world of

1. Paraphrased by Roheiser, quoted in Parker, "Ron Rolheiser Speaks on Grandiosity in Life."

2. Rolheiser, *Holy Longing*, 7.

Reason. Barbara had no spiritual context in which to frame her surprising experience. Her inductive mind, looking back through the years, remembers that she had very little sleep the night before, had not eaten much, and was dehydrated on that important day when she walked in Lone Pine and "saw the world—the mountains, the sky, the low scattered buildings—suddenly flame into life."[3]

In a *New York Times* op-ed piece, Barbara reaches back into her memory:

> There were no visions, no prophetic voices or visits by totemic animals, just this blazing everywhere. Something poured into me and I poured out into it. This was not the passive, beatific merger with "The All," as promised by the Eastern mystics. It was a furious encounter with a living substance that was coming at me through all things at once, too vast and violent to hold on to, too heartbreakingly beautiful to let go of. It seemed to me that whether you start as a twig or a gorgeous tapestry, you will be recruited into the flame and made indistinguishable from the rest of the blaze. I felt ecstatic and somehow completed, but also shattered.[4]

The philosopher William James would affirm that this was indeed a mystical encounter with a Presence: direct, noetic, life-changing, coming when least expected, ineffable. Words are inadequate to describe such an encounter; nevertheless, it represents a truth that deeply resonates within Barbara's total being.

She did not live in a world in which she could comfortably reflect on this experience. It was the world of the Enlightenment, a world of exclusive Reason: Rene Descartes' world of a buffered self, where spirits and unseen powers and strong emotions cannot get at the core of the person, where such talk is consigned to the dark recesses of superstition and folk religion. Her scientific training dismissed the experience, putting it down to a temporary mental breakdown as a result of chemical imbalance.

But noetic experiences like this get imbedded deep within our being and have the power to resurface in dreams and quiet moments of consciousness. In trying to figure out what happened to her those many years ago, Barbara became a student of world religions.

Surveys reveal that about half of the people in the United States claim to have had an experience such as Barbara's, a mystical experience. How

3. See below.
4. Ehrenreich, "Rationalist's Mystic Moment."

does a rational scientist and atheist make sense of such a mystical encounter? She put in this way in an interview in the *Los Angeles Times*:

> What do you do with something like this—an experience so anomalous, so disconnected from the normal life you share with other people . . . that you can't even figure out how to talk about it?[5]

Barbara Ehrenreich's in-depth response to this question is in her new book, *Living with a Wild God: A Nonbeliever's Search for the Truth About Everything*.

Her scientific training in inductive exploration and connection of data ironically led her to intense analysis of her experience, to name and to consider all the possibilities. What had she encountered in that mystical experience? The faithful scientist in her dismissed the all-encompassing, forceful, bright Presence of that day in Lone Pine as a mental aberration. But during her rigorous search for the truth about her own mystical experience, she became aware that neuroscientists were beginning to get in on the act. It was now possible to electronically scan and map the brain as a subject experienced mystical ecstasy. So, we are learning what areas of the brain light up when Tibetan monks and Roman Catholic nuns spend hours in deep meditation, and the physiological changes that take places in those brains. Are we "wired" for transcendent experience? Can the rigid dogmatism of science step back, and apply inductive detective tools to search out the source of mysterious experiences such as Barbara's? She reflects:

> There is no evidence for a God or gods, least of all caring ones, but our mystical experiences give us tantalizing glimpses of other forms of consciousness, which may be beings of some kind, ordinarily invisible to us and our instruments. Or it could be that the universe is itself pulsing with a kind of life, and capable of bursting into something that looks to us momentarily like the flame?[6]

Her new book is a critique of the dead world of Cartesian science. But more than that, it is to me tantalizing, perhaps exciting, in its implication that simply because a mystical experience might be elusive or impossible to describe it is bogus to dismiss it.

> How do we reconcile the mystical experience with daily life? Let us be open to the anomalous experience. If you see something that

---

5. Quoted in Ulin, "Barbara Ehrenreich Faces the Mystical."
6. Ehrenreich, "Rationalist's Mystic Moment."

looks like the Other, do not fall on your knees. Find out what it is and report back.[7]

I am thinking of my students in the classes on world religions that I have taught for over forty years. Indeed, I have dedicated this book to my students, who have played a great part in keeping me spiritually exercised (if not fit!) during those years. Many have grown up without a religious tradition; some were raised in a similar atheistic, skeptical family circle as described above. At the beginning of each year I try to help these students through their reactivity to religion per se, its institutional trappings and dark histories, to see that religion in its raw, native sense connects all of life together. I try to open my students' hearts to the possibility that we are indeed wired for mystical encounters with a Presence/the Other/the Holy, and that this connection is our deepest longing.

Sierra Nevada (Ansel Adams image), ca. 1943. County of Inyo, Eastern California Museum.

Some of my students can be quite vocal about their disbelief in God, which, though I greatly enjoy the discussions, to me is puzzling, as we will spend seventeen weeks exploring in-depth the passionate traditions of the world's religions. I ask whether they can describe this God in whom they cannot believe. I usually hear about disbelief in a stern, heavenly judge or

7. Ibid.

a capricious puppetmaster God. I can honestly respond that I don't believe in a God like that either.

These same students will acknowledge there could be some Presence out there somewhere, and indeed many have themselves had transformative encounters in nature.

Nicholas Lash, in his book *Theology for Pilgrims*, suggests that the God rejected by atheists is an idol of their own imaginations. Atheism does have a point in rejecting the existence of "A person without a body . . . eternal, free, able to do anything, knows everything . . . the proper object of human worship and obedience, the creator and sustainer of the universe."[8] However, if God can mean the mystery that created all things out of love and in wholeness, then all things live in a constant connection to the Presence, even if that relationship is not acknowledged. Lash contends that to make a decision to have nothing to do with this Presence is self-destructive.

Atheists help spiritual seekers identify the blind alleys of bad religion. In "The Value of Atheists," Ron Rolheiser reflects:

> They pick apart bad religion, showing us our blind spots, rationalizations, inconsistencies, double-standards, hypocrisies, moral selectivity, propensity for power, unhealthy fears, and hidden arrogance. Atheism shows us the log in our own eye.

How should believers in God respond to these honest criticisms of faith in God, even if these voices seem to feed off our religious faults? Rolheiser continues:

> Our response to atheism and criticism of our faith and religion should be threefold: First, we should be grateful for the challenge. We've never been fully faithful and we're better off openly hearing what's being thought of us and said of us than not hearing it. Denial is not a friend. Second, we have to acknowledge, without undue defensiveness, what's true and resist the temptation to defend ourselves in ways that simply create more bad religion for our critics to feed upon. When we're over-defensive before our critics, we not only cast ourselves and our churches in a bad light; worst of all, we cast God in a bad light. Finally, most important, the real response to bad religion is never secularism or atheism, but better religion! We need to be consistent, both in private conscience and in church practice.

8. Lash, *Theology for Pilgrims*, quoted in Rolheiser, "Ineffability of God."

Honest conversation with atheists helps Christians and other believers look at the limitations of their images of God, who is, after all, mystery beyond full comprehension.

Apophatic spirituality includes conversation about who God is *not*. Doubt and questions are part of a maturing faith. Often a personal crisis, a dark night of the soul, can bring transformation into a deep communion with the Other/God.

Even during my writing this book, our son Erik's many health crises have dragged our family through deserts of despair. Each day could be a different version of hell on earth. God—however we imagine God—can become for us just a memory of a distant presence. I would frequently find myself celebrating Mass, anointing the sick and dying, mouthing the liturgical words of a sacrament, though my heart of faith was not there. Many times the road could easily have led to the death of Erik. However, he lives, and each day is a gift. My retreats in Lone Pine and the eastern Sierra awakened a new awareness of God as a close, loving presence. Would I still have faith in God if I were going through the long grief of losing Erik? I don't know. But I do remember those foundational encounters with God. They are my spiritual ballast as I and we move into an unknown future.

I am thinking again about my students of world religions who either grew up without a religious tradition or who have had bad experiences with the religious establishment. They are reactive to traditional institutional language about spiritual experiences—and who could blame them? This is why Barbara Ehrenreich's inner work in processing her experience in Lone Pine without using monotheistic references is very helpful in my class, and makes sense of the larger context: that half the people in the United States claim some kind of mystical experience. Barbara acknowledges her upbringing in an atheistic, anti-religious family, and is clear about her exclusively secular education and its emphasis on strictly rational science. Yet she also acknowledges that she finds Cartesian methodological skepticism limited, especially when she tries to describe what happened to her in Lone Pine fifty years ago. She shares an expressive voice that can only help my students and others in integrating their own experiences with a Presence, the Other, the Holy, without resorting to the vocabulary and theology of traditional religion.

19

A Wounded Place

However excellent the day school may be, whatever the qualifications of the teacher, or however superior the facilities for instruction of the few short hours spent in the day school is, to a great extent, offset by the habits, scenes and surroundings of home—if a mere place to eat and live in can be called a home. Only by complete isolation of the Indian child from his savage antecedents can he be satisfactorily educated, and the extra expense attendant thereon is more than compensated by the thoroughness of the work.

—John B. Riley, Indian school superintendent[1]

Sprigs of Great Basin sage are tightly wrapped in string. The sacred bundle looks like a fat cigar. My new friend, Eric, a member of the Washoe Tribe of Carson City, Nevada, and an anthropology student at the University of Nevada at Reno, clicks his cigarette lighter alight. He holds the flame over the sage and blows on it gently and patiently. Smoke rises. I remove my hat as he gives me the sacred bundle. As I move the sage smoke up and down over the length of my body, in a circular motion around my head, fanning the smoke into my face, the words of Psalm 141 come forth: "Let our prayer come like incense before you."

The ritual is a necessary cleansing because I am standing in a wounded place. This is the site of the Stewart Indian School, which operated from 1890 to 1980. All around me are stone buildings from the late nineteenth century: classrooms, dormitories, and a dining hall, where Native American children lived and attended school. The U.S. Army had rounded them

---

1. In the 1886 *Annual Report of the Commissioner of Indian Affairs to the Secretary of the Interior*, quoted from Bear, "American Indian Boarding Schools Haunt Many."

136

up and brought them great distances, away from family and tribe, intentionally to disconnect them from traditional ways and give them the skills it was supposed they would need to live in the new European-American world. In these now boarded-up buildings spirits moan in longing for the old ways and the fading faces of distant family.

I am participating in the annual summer field school offered to anthropology students by the University of Nevada, Reno in partnership with the Nevada Indian Commission and the Washoe Tribal Historical Preservation Office. The class teaches the basic skills of field archaeology: how to lay out a site systematically, using mathematics and geo-positioning. This is the eighth field school in which I have participated. My friend Dr. Sarah Cowie is the site director. She can be seen patiently walking the sections where we are digging, offering a dialectic of probing questions, discussing, and helping the students reflect on where they are and precisely what it is they are looking at.

The dismal story of the relationship between European-American and Native American cultures is one of plunder and deception by the former against the latter. There are many instances of perhaps well-meaning but blundering archeologists and other scholars gaining the trust of tribal members in order to find out secrets about their traditions and possible locations for excavations, and then betraying that trust. As a result, the revered remains of ancestors have been disinterred and put on public display in museums. Even the hallowed halls of the Smithsonian Museum have collected examples. Only recently has there been some remediation of such desecration with the return of ancestral remains to their tribes and original resting places. So, you can understand that many Native Americans have learned to be deeply suspicious of the academics.

To me, Dr. Cowie is the perfect person for building new relationships of trust and respect. She brings years of experience working with tribes in Arizona, and has a genuine sensitivity for the concerns of Native Americans. During my visit this year, she met with leaders of the Indian Commission, which resulted in no fewer than ten Native American students signing on for the class. This was an intentional effort to build bridges and empower these students with academic skills for further the study of their heritage.

The Stewart Indian School opened in 1890 with a federal mandate to educate Indian children so they could work in European-American society. They learned household tasks so they could be employed in the towns, and trade skills such as shoemaking, blacksmithing, and plumbing. Speaking in their native tongue and practicing tribal traditions were forbidden to the pupils.

Author with Eric of Washoe Tribe, tribal elders in distance,
Stewart Indian School site, 2013. Author's collection.

In this desert where humidity is usually less than 5 percent and the sun burns starkly, it is a challenge to stay hydrated. I make it my business to offer the water jug to my youthful colleagues every few minutes. It is a new experience for me to be working closely with several Washoe Indian students in our area of the dig. We are on our knees together with trowels, scraping the hard clay and screening the very dusty debris through riddles. My screening partner is Eric, whose own grandmother was a pupil here. He tells me that there were good as well as bad things that happened at Stewart. He says his grandmother had mostly good memories of friendship with other students and the teachers. Eric himself is given to cheerful banter with me and the other students.

I lift the orange bucket filled with dirt from our excavation pit. Very heavy. I pour it into the screen being held up by Eric and he shakes the screen into a huge cloud of dust. We both sift around the remaining rocks and gravel on top of the screen, looking for anything unusual. Our finds are often about the size of my fingernail: a piece of charcoal, some wood, or a shard of glass. Our section is the site of a one-room wooden schoolhouse from the 1870s, which predates the other buildings. I see something tiny and square and lift it up. We look at it carefully. It is inscribed with strange designs. Eric thinks it is part of a bracelet, with tribal markings. He holds the item in the palm of his hand and sighs. What is he thinking and feeling?

I take a brown paper bag with our pit number and date written on it. What we have found today will go to the laboratory at the university. There will be cataloging and categorization and the data will be put on a computer. The Mind of Science that we have inherited from the Enlightenment labels these finds, composes the data, and makes a hypothesis of the construction and use of the wooden schoolhouse, which burned down in 1890. But to Eric this fragment of bracelet is sacred. In his tradition, all life is filled with spirit presence; even these pieces of rock are spirit-charged, because they are in a place that is part of his tribe's history.

Finding that fragment of bracelet with Eric changed my sense of presence in this place. In the past, archaeology removed valuable items, identified them, categorized them, and then stored them away in dusty warehouses to be available for future research. But every item we touched that day in this place is sacred and spirit-charged.

Most of my experience with Native American culture has been with the Owens Valley Paiute. I asked Eric if the Washoe people were part of the Northern Paiute and, boy, did he correct me! "Our people were here before the Paiute came. Our language is not Numic. We are *not* Paiute." I reflected with him about all the good social service programs that had been created by the Bishop Paiute Tribe, using their casino cash to benefit everyone. He said he had an old girlfriend who lived in Bishop and that place now had bad vibes for him. I suggested he bring a big bundle of sacred sage to Bishop and purify that place from the memories of his lost love. He gave a hearty laugh.

The senior student in our group was a lady of the Washoe Tribe who was completing her PhD. While we worked in the hot sun, screening the debris in a cloud of dust, tribal elders stood close by to observe. I could read in their faces a sense of pride in this new generation of university students reclaiming their culture and helping to heal a wounded place.

At the end of a long, hot desert day, searing sun having sucked the moisture from our parched bodies, we close up the excavation site. Holes are covered with plywood sheets and thick blue tarpaulins. The students cluster beneath the protective shade of a grand century-old cottonwood tree. I join them in the cool shade. A moist breeze creeps toward us from the Carson River.

After Sarah's reflection with the students on the discoveries of the day, during which she offered hypotheses about the meaning of what has been collected so far, most of the non-native students drift toward their cars. A group of Washoe students remain, however, talking with one of the tribal elders whom I had seen visiting the site earlier. She is speaking the tribal tongue, Wasiw. I had heard that the Washoe Tribe was focusing on language education with their youth, trying to save the tongue from extinction. I am indeed listening in on a language lesson. The elder patiently speaks a phrase, looks around the circle of native students, listens to the pronunciation from each person, and corrects as needed.

University of Nevada at Reno Anthropology Field School,
Stewart Indian School site, 2013. Author's collection.

As the summer sun sets behind the Sierra Nevada to the west, my gaze turns southward to Highway 395. I traveled that road three hundred miles to come to this place. My journey led me through numinous encounters with the Holy of the great variety of the world's spiritualties. At one time, this entire region, the Great Basin, was populated by native tribes, the First

People. As you and I have traveled this road together, meditating on the world religions, I see that underpinning every new expression of the Holy, and imbedded deep in this vast desert landscape, are the spirit presences of traditional religion. I conclude our journey at this northern end of Highway 395, in the company of native men and women who have been digging into sacred roots and learning the ancient voice of their people. While they are learning the mental processes of scientific thinking that the world has inherited from the Enlightenment, these students are not now an occupied and oppressed people. They are shaping themselves and empowering themselves to build an entirely different future. So, these young minds and hearts kindle hope for the future not only of their own people, but of all of us.

With my son, Erik, at Owens River, 2013. Author's collection.

Bibliography

Ali, Abdullah Yusuf. *The Meaning of the Holy Quran*. New edition with revised translation and commentary. Brentwood, MD: Amana, 1985.

Armor, John, et al. *Manzanar*. New York: Times Books, 1960. Includes iconic photographs by Ansel Adams and many others.

Aston, W. G. *Shinto: The Ancient Religion of Japan*. London: Constable, 1910.

Bahr, Diana Meyers. *Viola Martinez, California Paiute: Living in Two Worlds*. Norman: University of Oklahoma Press, 2003.

Bear, Charla. "American Indian Boarding Schools Haunt Many." NPR, News, May 12, 2008. Online: http://www.npr.org/templates/story/story.php?storyId=16516865.

Bellah, Robert N. *Habits of the Heart: Individualism and Commitment in American Life*. Berkeley: University of California Press, 1985.

Black Elk, and Joseph Epes Brown. *The Sacred Pipe: Black Elk's Account of the Seven Rites of the Oglala Sioux*. Norman: University of Oklahoma Press, 1989.

Bodine, Mike. "Pilgrimage to Honor Civil Rights Pioneers." *Inyo Register*, April 18, 2011. Online: http://www.inyoregister.com/node/1270.

Bray, Faustin. "Interview with the Sage: Faustin Bray Interviews Franklin Merrell-Wolff." Video. Sound Photosynthesis, 1982. Online: http://www.youtube.com/watch?v=BIMazReCp28.

Brueggemann, Walter. *The Land: Place as Gift, Promise and Challenge in Biblical Faith*. 2nd ed. Philadelphia: Fortress, 2002.

Bstan-'dzin-rgya-mtsho (Dalai Lama XIV). *Essence of the Heart Sutra: The Dalai Lama's Heart of Wisdom Teachings*. Translated and edited by Geshe Thupten Jinpa. Boston: Wisdom, 2002.

Buber, Martin. *I and Thou*. Translated by Ronald Gregor Smith. 2nd ed. New York: Continuum, 2004.

Burton-Christie, Douglas. *The Word in the Desert: Scripture and the Question for Holiness in Early Christian Monasticism*. Oxford: Oxford University Press, 1993.

California Cattlemen's Association. Online: http://www.calcattlemen.org/.

Carmody, Denise, and John Carmody. *Mysticism: Holiness East and West*. New York: Oxford University Press, 1996.

"Cave of Hira." Online: https://www.youtube.com/watch?v=RMq2mYXPdsk. Video of the Cave of Hira, where Muhammad received his revelation.

Chalfant, W. A. *The Story of Inyo*. Bishop, CA: Chalfant, 1975.

Clooney, Francis X. *Hindu Wisdom for All God's Children*. Maryknoll, NY: Orbis, 1998.

Colegate, Isabel. *A Pelican in the Wilderness: Hermits, Solitaries, and Recluses.* Berkeley, CA: Counterpoint, 2002.

"Day of the Dead." *Orange County Register*, November 1, 2012.

Eastern California Museum. Online: http://www.inyocounty.us/ecmuseum/.

Eastern Sierra Birding Trail Map. Online: http://www.easternsierrabirdingtrail.org/.

Eck, Diana. *Encountering God: A Spiritual Journey from Bozeman to Banaras.* Boston: Beacon, 1993.

Eck, Diana, and Kathryn Lohre. "The Role of Diversity in Pluralism." Video. Odyssey Networks, 2011. Online: http://www.youtube.com/watch?v=eiW7l2DG8zM.

Ehrenreich, Barbara. *Living with a Wild God: A Nonbeliever's Search for the Truth about Everything.* New York: Twelve, 2014.

———. "A Rationalist's Mystic Moment." *New York Times*, Opinion, April 5, 2014. Online: http://www.nytimes.com/2014/04/06/opinion/sunday/a-rationalists-mystical-moment.html.

Forstenzer, Martin. "Bitter Feelings Still Run Deep at Camp." *Los Angeles Times*, April 4, 1996. Online: http://articles.latimes.com/1996-04-04/news/mn-54883_1_manzanar-internment-camp.

Franklin Merrell-Wolff Fellowship. Online: http://www.merrell-wolff.org.

Funk, Will. "The Lost Water Gardens of Manzanar." *Splash* (magazine), July–August 2006, 88–97.

Fussell, Betty. *Raising Steaks: The Life and Times of American Beef.* Boston: Harcourt, 2008.

Grey, Zane. "The Man Who Influenced Me Most." *American Magazine*, August 1926, 52–55, 130–36.

Grey, Zane. *The Shepherd of Guadaloupe.* New York: Harper, 1930.

Hafiz. *The Gift: Poems by the Great Sufi Master.* Translated by Daniel Ladinsky. New York: Penguin, 1999.

Hagen, Stephen. *Buddhism: Plain and Simple.* London: Penguin, 1999. A clear explanation of the Four Noble Truths and the Eight-Fold Path. It appears that mystics, who have spent a lifetime in prayer and meditation, have a powerful sense of humor

Halik, Tomas. "Why Have You Forsaken Me?: Five Theses on Faith and Atheism." ABC Religion and Ethics, March, 18, 2014. Online: http://www.abc.net.au/religion/articles/2014/03/18/3965697.htm.

Hammarskjöld, Dag. *Markings.* Translated by Leif Sjöberg and W. H. Auden. New York: Knopf, 1964.

Hassel, David J. *Prayer of Reminiscence.* Chicago: Loyola University Press, 2007.

Hernandez, Wil. *Henri Nouwen and Spiritual Polarities: A Life of Tension.* New York: Paulist, 2012.

Hesse, Hermann. *Siddhartha.* Translated by Hilda Rosner. New York: Bantam, 1981.

Hulse, Ed. *Filming the West of Zane Grey.* Lone Pine, CA: Lone Pine Publishing, 2007.

Hussa, Linda. *The Family Ranch: Land, Children, and Tradition in the American West.* Reno: University of Nevada Press, 2009.

Ignatius Loyola. *The Spiritual Exercises of Saint Ignatius.* Translated by Anthony Mottola. New York: Doubleday, 1989. Japanese American National Museum. Online: http://www.janm.org/.

Johnson, Michael. *Hunger for the Wild: America's Obsession with the Untamed West.* Lawrence: University Press of Kansas, 2007.

Johnston, William. *Arise, My Love: Mysticism for a New Era.* Maryknoll, NY: Orbis, 2000.

————. *Silent Music: The Science of Meditation.* San Francisco: Harper & Row, 1974. Father Johnston, SJ, has spent most of his life in Asia studying the connections between Zen meditation and Christianity. He says, "Zen taught me how to pray as a Christian."

Jones, Robert A., editor. *The Essential Henri Nouwen.* San Francisco: Shambhala, 2009.

Jung, Carl G. *Memories, Dreams, Reflections.* New York: Vintage, 1963.

Karelius, Brad. *The Spirit in the Desert: Pilgrimages to Sacred Sites in the Owens Valley.* Laguna Niguel, CA: Desert Spirit, 2010. Includes a detailed topography of Walker and Olancha Creeks and other sites.

Keating, Thomas. *Open Mind, Open Heart: The Contemplative Dimension of the Gospel.* New York: Continuum, 2006.

Kerekez, Alex. "Ancient Paiute Indian Camp." Videos of a Paiute camp in the Fish Slough area of Owens Valley, Bishop, CA. 2 episodes. Online: http://www.youtube.com/watch?v=6HcfbFMDtRE and http://www.youtube.com/watch?v=Wn9uSXVZZZY.

KQED. "This Week: This Is Us: Manzanar." Online: http://www.youtube.com/watch?v=iuY8f8kKvro.

Krause, Bernie. "Discovering a 'Singing' Tree." California Academy of Sciences, San Francisco, CA, September 22, 2009.

FORA.tv. Online: https://www.youtube.com/watch?v=uWkMWDSVZuQ. Video of Krause explaining how he recorded audio signals emitting from the trunk of a cottonwood tree while trying to record bat emissions.

Küng, Hans, Josef Van Ess, Heinrich Von Stietencron, and Heinz Bechert. *Christianity and World Religions: Paths of Dialogue with Islam, Hinduism, and Buddhism.* Translated by Peter Heinegg. Maryknoll, NY: Orbis, 1993.

Lacey, Brenda. "Calving Season." Lacey Family Ranch Blog, March 22, 2011. Online: http://californiafamilyranching.blogspot.com/2011/03/calving-season.html.

Lane, Belden. "Galesville and Sinai: The Researcher as Participant in the Study of Spirituality and Sacred Space." *Christian Spirituality Bulletin* 23 (Spring 1994) 18–25.

————. *Landscapes of the Sacred: Geography and Narrative in American Spirituality.* Expanded ed. Baltimore, MD: Johns Hopkins University Press, 2001.

Langley, Chris. "Living in the Land of 20 Mile Shadows." *Territorial Review Monthly,* November 2008.

Lash, Nicholas. *Theology for Pilgrims.* London: Darton, Longman & Todd, 2008.

Littleton, C. Scott. *Shinto: Origins, Rituals, Festivals, Spirits, Sacred Places.* Oxford: Oxford University Press, 2002.

Lone Pine Film History Museum. Online: http://www.lonepinefilmhistorymuseum.org.

MacKenzie, Scott. "Roadside Crosses: Personal Shrines in Public Places." *The Christian Century,* July 12, 2011, 11–12.

Maharshi, Ramana. *Who Am I? (Nan Yar?).* Translated by T. M. P. Mahadevan. Tiruvannamalai, South India: Sri Ramanasramam, n.d. Online: http://www.arunachala.org/elibrary/docs/who-ai/who-am-i/.

The Manzanar Committee. "Our Pilgrimage." Online: http://www.manzanarcommittee.org/The_Manzanar_Committee/Our_Pilgrimage.html.

————. "35th Annual Manzanar Pilgrimage (2004) – Part 7." Video of part 1 of the traditional interfaith service of the 35th Annual Manzanar Pilgrimage, April 24, 2004. Online: http://www.youtube.com/watch?v=uxNlw15hdzs.

Martin, James. *The Jesuit Guide to (Almost) Everything: A Spirituality for Real Life.* New York: HarperCollins, 2010. Pages 95–103 present a helpful outline of the Examination of Conscience, a meditation reviewing the events and people encountered daily. The process fosters gratitude for God's grace and awareness of God's presence in our lives.

Marutschke, Moritz. "Karesansui: Incorporation of Japanese Spirit and Nature." *Kyoto This Month* (*Kyoto Visitor's Guide*), March 2013. Online: http://www.kyotoguide. com/ver2/thismonth/Karesansui.html.

Mascaro, Juan, translator. *The Upanishads*. New York: Penguin, 1965.

May, Gerald G. *Addiction and Grace: Love and Spirituality in the Healing of Addictions*. San Francisco: HarperSanFrancisco, 1991.

———. *The Wisdom of Wilderness: Experiencing the Healing Power of Nature*. New York: HarperCollins, 2006.

McCauley, Michael. "The Deep Mystery of God." *America*, October 18, 2004. Online: http://americamagazine.org/issue/500/article/deep-mystery-god.

McCluhan, T. C. *Touch the Earth: A Self-Portrait of Indian Existence*. London: Abacus, 1980.

McFarlane, Thomas J. "The Nondual Philosophy of Franklin Merrell-Wolff." Online: http://www.intergalscience.org/gsc/.

McMahon, Jennifer, and Steve Csaki. *The Philosophy of the Western*. Lexington: University Press of Kentucky, 2010.

Merton, Thomas. *New Seeds of Contemplation*. New York: New Directions, 2007.

———. *The Way of Chuang Tzu*. New York: New Directions, 1963.

Mitchell, Stephen, translator. *Tao Te Ching*. By Lao Tzu. A new English version with foreword and notes. San Francisco: Harper Perennial, 2009.

Multerland. "Spiritual Poetry: Tao Te Ching, Lao Tzu ~ chapter 1 (Meditation about Tao)." Meditation video. Online: http://www.youtube.com/watch?v=VB3PH5j6oOg.

Nash, James A. *Loving Nature: Ecological Integrity and Christian Responsibility*. Nashville: Abingdon, 1991.

National Park Service. "Manzanar." Online: http://www.nps.gov/manz/index.htm.

Nerburn, Ken. *Neither Wolf, Neither Dog: On Forgotten Roads with an Indian Elder*. Novato, CA: New World Library, 2002.

Nouwen, Henri. "Being the Beloved." Message delivered for *Hour of Power*, episode 1177. Crystal Cathedral, Garden Grove, CA, 1993. Online: http://www.youtube.com/ watch?v=v8U4V4aaNWk.

———. *The Essential Henri Nouwen*. Edited by Robert A. Jonas. Boston: Shambhala, 2009.

Ono, Sokyo. *Shinto: The Kami Way*. Boston: Tuttle, 2004.

Orenstein, Peggy. "The Way We Live Now: I Tweet, Therefore I Am." *New York Times Magazine*, August 1, 2010. Online: http://www.nytimes.com/2010/08/01/ magazine/01wwln-lede-t.html.

Parker, J. Michael. "Ron Rolheiser Speaks on Grandiosity in Life." *Today's Catholic*, June 2014. Reproduced online at: http://ronrolheiser.com/me/uploads/2014/07/ RONROL-todayscatholic-web.pdf.

Pennington, M. Basil. *True Self/False Self: Unmasking the Spirit Within*. New York: Crossroads, 2000.

Pennington, M. Basil, Thomas Keating, and Thomas E. Clarke. *Finding Grace at the Center: The Beginning of Centering Prayer*. Woodstock, VT: SkyLight Paths, 2007.

Proust, Marcel. *The Guermantes Way*. Vol. 3 of *In Search of Lost Time*. Translated by C. K. Scott Moncrieff and Terence Kilmartin. London: Everyman, 2001.

"The Reward Mine." Video of the Reward Mine, near Lone Pine, CA. Online: http://www. youtube.com/watch?v=mDzdYq93zZs.

Rilke, Rainer Maria. *Ahead of All Parting: The Selected Poetry and Prose of Rainer Maria Rilke.* Translated by Stephen Mitchell. New York: Modern Library, 1995.

Rolheiser, Ron. *The Holy Longing: The Search for a Christian Spirituality.* New York: Doubleday, 1998.

———. "Atheism and Belief." November 14, 2010. Online: http://ronrolheiser.com/atheism-and-belief/.

———. "The Desert: A Place of Preparation." March 12, 2000. Online: http://ronrolheiser.com/the-desert-a-place-of-preparation/.

———. "The Desert – The Place of God's Closeness." April 2, 2000. Online: http://ronrolheiser.com/the-desert-the-place-of-gods-closeness/.

———. "The Domestic Monastery." January 7, 2001. Online: http://ronrolheiser.com/the-domestic-monastery/.

———. "The Ineffability of God." January 13, 2013. Online: http://ronrolheiser.com/the-ineffability-of-god/.

———. "The Language of Silence." January 28, 2007. Online: http://ronrolheiser.com/the-language-of-silence/.

———. "Longing for Solitude." July 1, 2012. Online: http://ronrolheiser.com/longing-for-solitude/.

———. "The Major Points of Convergence within the Great Spiritual Traditions." April 19, 2009. Online: http://ronrolheiser.com/the-major-points-of-convergence-within-the-great-spiritual-traditions/.

———. "The Value of Atheists." September 1, 2013. Online: http://ronrolheiser.com/the-value-of-atheists/.

Rummelsburg, Steven Jonathan. "The Real St. Anthony." *The Integrated Catholic Life,* January 17, 2015. Online: http://www.integratedcatholiclife.org/2015/01/rummelsburg-the-real-st-anthony/.

Russell, Norman. *The Lives of the Desert Fathers: The Historia Monachorum in Aegypto.* London: Cistercian, 1980.

Sahagun, Louis. "In California's Backcountry, Seeking Movie Backdrops." *Los Angeles Times,* April 29, 2013. Online: http://www.latimes.com/local/la-me-movie-museum-20130429-dto-htmlstory.html. Article and video about the Lone Pine Film History Museum.

Schimmel, Annemarie. *And Muhammad Is His Messenger: The Veneration of the Prophet in Islamic Piety.* Chapel Hill: University of North Carolina Press, 1985.

Sheldrake, Philip. *Spaces for the Sacred: Place, Memory, and Identity.* Baltimore: John Hopkins University Press, 2001.

Shelley, Percy Bysshe. *The Selected Poetry and Prose of Shelley.* Ware: Wordsworth, 2002.

Silko, Leslie Marmon. *The Turquoise Ledge: A Memoir.* New York: Viking-Penguin, 2010.

Smith Thomas, Heather. *Storey's Guide to Raising Beef Cattle.* North Adams, MS: Storey Books, 1998.

Steinmetz, Paul. *Meditations with the Lakota: Prayers, Songs, and Stories of Healing and Harmony.* Rochester, VT: Bear, 2001.

Swindells, John. *A Human Search: Bede Griffiths Reflects on His Life.* Liguori, MS: Triumph, 1997.

Takei, Jiro, and Marc P. Keane. *Sakuteiki: Visions of the Japanese Garden.* Tokyo: Tuttle, 2008.

Tanner, Stephen L. "Spiritual Values in the Popular Western Novel." *Literature and Belief* 21/1, 2 (2001).

Taylor, Charles. *A Secular Age.* Cambridge, MA: Belknap Press of Harvard University Press, 2007.

Tracy, David. *On Naming the Present: Reflections on God, Hermeneutics, and Church.* Maryknoll, NY: Orbis, 1994.

Toolan, David. *At Home in the Cosmos.* Maryknoll, NY: Orbis, 2001.

Ubbina, Ian. "Roadside Memorials." *New York Times*, February 6, 2006.

Ulin, David L. "Barbara Ehrenreich Faces the Mystical in 'Living With a Wild God.'" *Los Angeles Times*, April 4, 2014. Online: http://articles.latimes.com/2014/apr/04/entertainment/la-ca-jc-barbara-ehrenreich-20140406.

Vandewege. John. "Statues of Faith in the Desert." Online: http://www.youtube.com/watch?v=Dz1a6S77iu4. Video interview of Buddhist monk Thich Dang "Tom" Phap.

Vivekananda, Swami. *The Complete Works of Swami Vivekananda.* Vol. 2. Calcutta, India: Advaita Ashrama, 2009.

Voragine, Jacobus de. *The Golden Legend.* Vol. 2. Translated by William Caxton, edited by F. S. Ellis. 1900. Online: http://www.ccel.org/ccel/voragine/goldleg2.

Wakatsuki, Jeanne, and James D. Houston. *Farewell to Manzanar.* New York: Houghton Mifflin, 1973.

Weber, Max. *The Protestant Ethic and the Spirit of Capitalism.* Edited and translated by Peter Baehr and Gordon C. Wells. New York: Penguin, 2002.

Wehrey Jane. *Voices From This Long Brown Land: Oral Recollections of Owens Valley Lives and Manzanar Pasts.* New York: Palgrave-Macmillan, 2006. A disturbing and honest encounter with the oppression of Native American culture in the past, giving hope for the future.

Yusuf Ali, Abdullah, translator. *The Meaning of the Holy Qur'an.* New ed. with rev. translation. Brentwood, MD: Amana, 1991.

Index of Names

A

Abraham, 54, 55, 57
Abu Bahr, 56
Adam, 55, 57
Adams, Ansel, 95, 96
Ali, Abdullah Yusuf, 25n1, 51n1, 55n2
Anthony, Saint, 128
Appah, 59
Arnold, J. R., 96–97
Arnold, Marie Carillo, 96–97
Aston, W. G., 87n1
Augustine, Saint, 82, 85
Autry, Gene, 108

B

Bacon, Francis, 75
Bear, Charla, 136n1
Bechert, Heinz, 34n5
Becker, Father Ed, 3, 4
Bellah, Robert, 77
Bellas, Chappo, *104*
Biano, Ochwiay, 73
Black Elk, 31, 31n2
Bodin, Mike, 92n6
Bray, Faustin, 121n7
Brown, Joseph Epes, 31n2
Brueggemann, Walter, 9, 9n3
Buber, Martin, 33–34, 33n12, 42
Buddha, 15–16, 66

Budner, Lawrence, 63
Burkhardt, Fred, *104*
Butcherknife, Chief, 39

C

Chalfant, W. A., 39, 39n3
Chappel, Gordon, 91n5
Confucius, 41
Cooper, Gary, 110
Cordova, Rudy, 87, 87n2
Cowie, Sarah, 137, 140

D

Dali Lama, 18, 24
Day, Dorthy, 129
De Niro, Robert, 123–124
Descartes, René, 75, 131
Doughty, Lieutenant, 39
Downey, Robert, Jr., 108
Duvall, Robert, 124

E

Eck, Diana, 20–21
Eckhart, Meister, 37
Edwards, Danielle, 5

M

MacIntyre, Cardinal, 65
Madison, James, 76
Maharishi, Ramana, 119n5
Mary, mother of Jesus, 9, 16, 57
Mascaro, Juan, 113n2
May, Gerald, 62, 62n4, 99, 99n1, 103,
      103n34, 104, 104n5
McCauley, Michael, 42n6–47, 43n8
McKenna, Corporal, 39
McLuhan, T. C., 36, 36n6
McNerney, Sister Eileen, 113
Melton, Thomas, 24
Merrill-Wolff, Franklin, 120, 120–122
Merrill-Wolff, Sherifa, 120, 122
Merritt, Ralph, 95
Merton, Thomas, 15, 23, 23n56, 49, 69,
      69n10
Mitchell, Stephen, 41n4, 42n5, 43n9
Mohammed, 54–56
Moon, Kelly, 6, 7
Moreland, Fr. Gordon, 82, 82n1, 86
Moses, 42, 56, 61, 84
Murdock, Martin, 65

N

Nash, James, xii
Nishi, Barbara, 95
Nishi, Edith, 95
Nishi, Henry, 95
Nishi, Kuichiro, 94–95, 97, 98, 104
Noah, 55, 57
Norinaga, 87
Nouwen, Fr. Henri, 46, 46n1, 126, 127,
      127n2
Nunn, L. L., 58, 58n1

O

Ono, Sokyo, 90n4

P

Parker, J. Michael, 130n1
Peck, Gregory, 110
Pennington, M. Basil, 65, 65n5, 67
Phap, Thich Dang "Tom," 13, 17, 18
Phillips, Robert, 60–62, 64, 65–66
Pino, Paul, 6, 7
Plato, 66, 130
Proust, Marcel, 1, 1n1

Q

Quan Yin, 11, 11n1, 12–14, 16, 18

R

Riley, John B., 136
Rilke, Rainer Maria, 117, 117n4
Rogers, Roy, 108
Rolheiser, Fr. Ron, 23, 37, 37n12, 44,
      44n10, 48, 49, 49n2, 50n34, 66–
      67, 66n67, 67n8, 111, 129, 129n4,
      130, 130n12, 134, 134n8
Roosevelt, Franklin, 91
Rousseau, Jean-Jacques, 110
Rusack, Robert C., 124

S

Sakuteiki, 96–97
Sarah, 54
Schimmel, Annemarie, 55n3
Scott, Randolph, 110
Shelley, Percy Bysshe, 123, 123n1
Sherman, Colonel, 38
Shirley, Jim, 5
Siddhartha Gautama, 15–16, 61
Silko, Leslie Marmon, 70, 70n1
Smith, Fr. Christopher, 3
Smith, Huston, 118
Steinmetz, Fr. Paul, 77, 77n5
Stietencron, Heinrich von, 34

T

Tanner, Stephen L., 110, 110n3
Taylor, Charles, 74, 75, 75n4
Thomas Aquinas, 42
Thoreau, Henry David, 110
Toolan, David, 116–117, 117n3
Tracey, David, 19, 19n3
Trever, John, 64
Tzu, Lao. *See* Lao Tzu

U

Ulin, David L., 132n5
Upanishad, Mandukya, 113

V

Van Ess, Josef, 34n5
Vivekananda, Swami, 119, 119n6
Voragine, Jacobus de, 128n3

W

Wakatsuki, Jeanne, 88, 88n3, 94, 94n1
Wayne, John, 58, 110
Weber, Max, 76
Wister, Owen, 110
Wolff, Franklin. *See* Merrill-Wolff, Franklin

Subject Index

Page numbers in *italic* type indicate photographs.

Berkeley, California, 64–65
Bhakti Yoga, 119
Biano, Ochwiay, 73–74
Bible
    translations of, 56
    as Word of God, 74–75
    See also Scripture references
Big Pine Paiute Indian Reservation, 79
bird-watching, 25, 29
Bishop Paiute Indian Reservation, 79
Black Elk, 31
Blessing of the Streets, 3–4
Blood Highway, 4
Blue Lake, 71
bodhisattvas, 16. *See also* Kuan Yin
    Bodhisattva (Compassionate
    Mother)
Brahman/God
    experience of merging with, 34
    as Only Truth, 118
    as ultimate reality, 116
    union with atman, 15, 34, 116,
        118–119
    union with through yoga, 118–120
Braunschweig, Germany, 113–114
Brueggemann, Walter, 9
Buber, Martin, 33–34, 42
The Bucket List (film), 113
Buddha, 15, 16, 66
Buddhism
    birth of compared to Great
        Awakening (US), 14–15
    Four Noble Truths and Eightfold
        Path, 16
    geophysical divination with garden
        stones, 98
    importation into United States, 77,
        116
    Kuan Yin, 12–18
    in Southern California, 8
    state of prayer, 13
    transience of human experience as
        insight of, 30
    See also Zen Buddhism
Buddhists, 93
Budner, Lawrence, 63
buffered self, 75–76, 77, 131

busyness, 48–49, 50, 111
Butcherknife (Paiute chief), 39

C

California
    religious diversity of, 8
    seasons in, 1
    See also Highway 101; Highway 395;
        specific site in Owens Valley
California Aqueduct, 100
California Native plant Society,
    Bristlecone chapter, 80
California Trail, 6–7
"Canticle of the Sun" (St. Francis), 28–29
car crashes. *See* auto accidents
Carson and Colorado Railroad, 47–48
cattle, *100, 102*
    along the highway, 47
    birthing of, 101–102, 115
    branding time, *104*
    introduction into California, 79,
        100–101
    training of, 103–105
cattle drives, 7
cave of Hira, 54–56
cemeteries
    construction of in California, 7
    at Manzanar internment camp,
        90–91, *92*
Center for Spiritual Development,
    Orange, California, 67
centering prayer, 44, 67
Chalfant, W. A., 39
charcoal kilns, 38
childhood neighborhood, 94
Chinese gardens, 96–97
Chinese immigrants, 8
Chisholm Trail, 7
Christianity
    Great Awakening (1960s, US), 14–15,
        77, 116, 122
    Islam and, 56
    remembrance of the dead, 9
    revelation of Jesus, 29
Christians, 93

revealed in creation, 29
search for communion with, 15
speech through desert's voice, 58
sun as, 73
transformation of men in the desert,
    37
transformative communion with, 114
See also Allah; Brahman/God; Jesus
    Christ
Goffman, Erving, 69
gold, 51
gold mining, 7, 28, 47, 48, 79
Gospels, 116
gratitude
    at DeDecker Native Plant Garden, 80
    expressing during Examen of
        Consciousness, 68
    finding in solitude of Cottonwood
        Canyon, 39
    finding in the desert, 82–86
    as foundation of hope, 82, 86
    generosity associated with, 83
    memories evoking, 83–85, 127
    roadside memorials evoking, 10
Great Awakening (1960s, US), 14–15, 77,
    116, 122
great migration (early 1850s), 6–7
Grey, Loren, 107
Grey, Zane, 106–108, *109*, 110
grieving process, 5–6
Grosbard, Ulu, 123–124, *125*
Gunga Din (film), 109
gurus, 15

H

Habits of the Heart (Bellah), 77
Hafiz (Sufi mystic), 57
Hagar, 54
Hammarskjöld, Dag, 19, 113
Harlan, Roberta, 128
Hassel, David, SJ, 82, 85
hawks, 78
Hebrew people's wilderness experience,
    84
Heimbs family, 114

Hesse, Hermann, 19
Highway 91, 11–12
Highway 101, 7–8
Highway 395
    to base camp on Mount Whitney,
        58, 108
    to Carson City, Nevada, 31–32
    to Cottonwood Canyon, 37–39
    deadliest section of, 4, 18
    going east from to Reward Mine, 51
    Kuan Yin statue on roadside, 12–13,
        14
    Manzanar Japanese American
        Relocation Camp on, 87
    to Onion Valley, 79
    to Paiute Reservations, 78–79
    past Kramer Junction, xi
    to Reward Mine, 47–48
    roadside shrines along, 4–10
    to University of Nevada at Reno
        Anthropology Field School, 140
    urban encroachment along, 12
    vista points on, 30
    volcanic reefs on way to Little Lake,
        25
Hijrah Migration, 56
Hinduism
    birth of Buddhism and, 14–15
    importation into United States, 77,
        116
    meditation with yoga as tenet of, 66
    morning prayer, 59
    state of prayer, 13
Hindu temples, 8
Hindu yogi, 34
hiraniwa (flat gardens), 97
Holy Communion, 71–72, 74
The Holy Longing (Rolheiser), 48–49,
    66, 67
hope, 82, 86
Hopi, 32, 36
hour of death, 1
householder stage of life, 122
Houston, Jeanne Wakatsuki, 88
human experience, 1, 30
humanism, 76–77
hungry ghosts, 9, 88, 91

I

J

K

as aid to understanding Christianity, 23
answer to war-torn China, 41–42
Heavenly Immortals of, 97
image of alchemy and eternal life, 12
importation into United States, 77
veneration of the dead, 8, 9
Zen Buddhism and, 44
Taos Pueblo, New Mexico, 71
Tao Te Ching (Lao Tzu), 41, 42
Taylor, Charles, 74, 75
Technological Man, 77
temptation, 24, 123–129
Territorial Review Monthly, 121
thanksgiving, 68
Theology for Pilgrims (Lash), 134
Theravada Buddhism, 16
thin places
  at dawn, 58–59
  defined, 1
  in Owens Valley, 9
  roadside memorials as, 9–10
  shamans' penetration of, 78
  See also desert; solitude
Thomas Aquinas, 42–43
Thoreau, Henry David, 110
Tommyknockers, 53
toni nobe circular shelters, 81
Toolan, David, SJ, 116–117
TORCH screen, 89
Touch the Earth (McLuhan), 36
Tracy, David, 19
Trail of Tears (California), 79
Tremors (film), 108
Trever, John, 64
True Confessions (Grosbard film), 123–124
True Self
  author's finding of, 67, 126
  communion with God as path to, 67–68
  desert fostering, 69
  found in Jesus, 23
  Jesus' wrestling with in wilderness, 126
  meditation as path to, 67
  Merton's path to, 69

path to embracing, 61
yoga as path to, 118–119
See also Atman
tsukiyama (hill gardens), 97

U

UCLA Taiko Drummers, 91
unconditional love, 67
union with God/everything else, 23–24
University of Nevada at Reno Anthropology Field School, 32, 137–141, *140*
University of Southern California, 63–64, 85
Upanishad, Mandukya, 113
Upanishads, 15, 116
urban encroachment, 11–12
urbanization, 91
U.S. Army, 136–137
US Calvary, 79

V

"The Values of Atheists" (Rolheiser), 134
Vedic Hinduism, 14–15
veneration of the dead, 8
Vietnamese parishioners, 9
Vietnamese shrine, 12–18, *14*
vigils, 2
Virgin Mary. *See* Mary (mother of Jesus)
Visions of the Japanese Garden (Sakuteiki), 96
Vivekachudamani, the Crest Jewel, 118
Vivekananda, Swami, 119

W

Wakatsuki, Jeanne, 94
Walker Creek, 83
Wandering of the Wasteland (Grey), 108, 110
War Relocation Authority, 91
Warring States period, China, 41